WALTER HAMILTON

WALTER HAMILTON

1908–1988

A Portrait

Edited by Donald Wright

ISBN 0 907383 297
© Jane Hamilton 1992
First published 1992
Reprinted 1992

Typeset by Action Typesetting Limited
Printed by Antony Rowe Ltd, Chippenham, Wiltshire

Published by
James & James (Publishers) Limited
75 Carleton Road
London N7 0ET

ACKNOWLEDGEMENTS

THIS BOOK WAS the brainchild of Jock Burnet, who as Bursar of Magdalene worked closely with Walter throughout his years as Master and was one of his closest friends. Had it not been for him it is unlikely to have been born alive. The book is the poorer for his loss: he would undoubtedly have been one of its principal contributors. Three other old friends also died before the portrait's preparation had begun – Archie Nicholson, Tim Morony and Tom Howarth. Each would have had important and varied things to say.

The names of those whom I consulted appear at the end of the book. I am grateful to them all. Some may find little evidence to suggest the part they played was of value, but I would wish to disabuse them of that. All contributed to the shape or colour of the work.

I also wish to acknowledge with thanks the Governing Bodies' Association and the Headmasters' Conference for having allowed me to read the minutes of their meetings when Walter was Chairman, the Editor of the *Magdalene College Magazine and Record* for permission to publish from its obituary, and the Evening Standard Company Ltd for its article about Walter from his time at Westminster.

However, my special thanks and appreciation must be reserved for those who accepted the challenging task of assembling and writing the book's chapters, from collected material or personal knowledge. So far as possible the book

ACKNOWLEDGEMENTS

has been the work of eye-witnesses. Fortunately, Walter has contributed most of all, allowing those who knew him an opportunity to 'hear' him talking again. Three Addresses which he gave are published as an appendix. If anyone would like to read more than are included here copies could be made available.

I first came to know Walter at Shrewsbury, when he became Chairman of its Governing Body. Over the next thirteen years he became a very good friend of that School, which he had long respected. Yet the discovery of him in these pages has for me come as a revelation of a great life, and Jane Hamilton's invitation to make that discovery, and to present it for others, has been an extraordinary privilege. As for the assistance she and her family have given, it has been nothing less than a joy.

Coulston,   D.W.
Wiltshire.

CONTENTS

LIST OF PLATES

FOREWORD

Writing to me about this book its editor Donald Wright says, 'As time has gone on it has become a celebration'. And so it is, and rightly so. We are celebrating the life of someone whose appearance and expressed outlook on life were often wreathed in gloom, but who was one of the happiest men I have known. The paradox is there in each of the chapters which follow, and resolved in Walter's own pithy sermon on Happiness which is rightly included as an Appendix. I shall not try to rival Brian Young's masterly introduction. I glimpsed enough of Walter's life during most of the periods here described to relish the account given by each friend who knew each period better.

Walter Hamilton taught me at Eton, like so many others. We carry away much more than frayed memories of Latin and Greek verse. In my case he helped to form the tastes of a shy and abrupt boy. On Sunday evenings latecomers sat on the floor in his study as he read and lingered over Jane Austen and Trollope. We relished and now remember the dreadful moment when Mrs Proudie's ballroom dress was torn and she exclaimed 'Unhand it Sir'. We learned of his secret passion for Wodehouse. We looked forward to the sessions of 'secular singing' where he rendered out of tune and with deep melancholy the great Victorian ballads 'The Golden Picture' and the 'Bonnie Earl of Moray'.

The West Highland mixture of continuous hospitality, a leisurely and huge tolerance of eccentricity, provided for

Walter just the right balance against the austere and necessarily regimented life of a schoolmaster and don. Shark-fishing with Gavin Maxwell on the Minch, Château Yquem in profusion, Monopoly, extraordinary golf in the rain, sunsets over Skye, gossip, a constant coming and going of young and old – there is much happiness to remember under the roof of the Shaw Stewart family. As his daughter Caroline tells, Walter later created with Jane and his children his own version of West Highland life and there on Mull the happiness was prolonged.

Brian Young describes what Walter Hamilton achieved at Eton, Westminster and Rugby, at Trinity and at Magdalene. Recently I came across a letter which he wrote me from Rugby in 1965, which is typical of the way he talked about his work. 'This has been a fearful year, because I have been brought back to be Chairman of the Headmasters' Conference again, and am due to go on with this till the end of 1966. You can imagine what it's like with everybody having the jitters about the future of the public schools. I constantly repeat to myself Hamlet's lines, "The time is out of joint – O cursed spite, that ever *I* was born to set it right".' This kind of diffidence was normal, but behind it he was as strong as a rock. The public schools and ancient universities have much cause for gratitude to Walter, who was a more effective critic and champion precisely because he started from outside their familiar traditions.

More important is the debt so many of us, now elderly or middle-aged, feel to Walter as a guide, a friend, and an opener of doors. This book explains the debt, and so perhaps begins to repay it.

DOUGLAS HURD

INTRODUCTION

Brian Young

FOR A THOUSAND and more men the name 'Walter' evokes
just one mental picture; and many of them, on hearing it,
plunge immediately into a story or an imitation. A few of
these have searched their memories – and sometimes the
records too – in order to give words to that strong image in
the mind. A number of others will know, when they read the
words 'Walter Hamilton. A Portrait' that they want, as he
might say, to bask here in a little nostalgia. But those to
whom he was only a name might wonder why he, among
many schoolmasters, merits the distinction of being recalled
in a full book. This introduction tries to give an answer, as
it singles out some of the traits which made Walter Hamilton
so memorable and so attractive.

Any list of Walter's qualities must begin with his powerful
intelligence. Initially this enabled him to achieve swift
academic success: within the decade after taking School
Certificate, he began the study of Greek, won a classical
scholarship to Trinity, Cambridge, and was elected to a
fellowship for what he called 'becoming rather an expert on
Hell'. He also quickly developed as a felicitous composer of
Greek and Latin verse: I recall that, in his version of the
dialogue between Bosola and Antonio ('We are merely the
stars' tennis-balls'), perfection in the writing of Greek
iambics was made to seem a simple matter. But it was not to
scholarship alone that he devoted his sharp mind. He had
extraordinary skill at adapting himself to new environments:

only a man of keen intelligence and perception could have made himself, despite a certain shyness, so fully at home from the start both at Trinity and at Eton. His intelligence also gave him a vivid realisation of how others were feeling, so that he had a ready sympathy for those who were suffering setback or failure and an immediate understanding of those who called on him for advice. In his later years chairmanship – which is nothing more than applied intelligence – saw him grasping at once what mattered in a debate. Here then was a mind of high distinction. Not all of it was displayed, for he preferred to keep it in reserve; but those who were more articulate or more flashy sensed it in the background – he might well have remarked, as Melbourne did to Russell, 'I hope you've said nothing dam' foolish; I thought you were teeming with some imprudence yesterday.'

His mind was not only acute: it was also orderly. You can afford to be casual on the surface if you have confidence in a controlled pattern of work and life deeper down. Walter was very well organised and his mind was tidy and swept. An outward sign of this was the directness, the absence of waffling, in what he said and wrote. Less visible was the immensely heavy load he carried successfully in wartime as Master-in-College. It was his task to look after seventy bright and often difficult boys; to keep friendship in good repair with as many old boys (he wrote all his letters individually and by hand); to rise above the sadnesses of war and his occasional ill-health (he had unacknowledged whooping-cough throughout one Half); and to teach Sixth Form and pupils (a very onerous duty at Eton in those days). All this would have reduced to chaos anyone who lacked a systematic mind. Later, when he was a headmaster, the same clarity and orderliness of mind made him a skilful, and unshowy, administrator: pithy and decisive comments or letters showed him fully in command of any question that arose.

Brains he had, and moral force too. This also was not

much on display: high prating was not his line. But the brief sentence 'It won't do' marked a clear recognition of right and wrong. The Americans have a phrase which says of someone that he worries more about the sizzle than about the steak. Walter was the exact opposite. His Christian faith was communicated to boys without any religiosity: they felt that belief must be intellectually and emotionally respectable if someone of Walter's calibre was sure that it mattered and yet treated it undemonstratively and, when necessary, with humour. All this made him a man to be trusted. You might not actually go tiger-shooting with him, for such pursuits would not be to his taste, but he was certainly a man to have at your side if tigers uninvited were to gather round.

Yet (this indeed is the place for an 'At enim' if you learnt Latin prose from Walter) intelligence, system and moral certainty might be held to be a mark of many headmasters. Walter had a much more individual gift – a style that is well remembered by those who knew him. Some have compared this style to that of Eeyore, but this does not fully cover it. There was the deep voice; the accent that was not redolent of Oxbridge; the low and even timbre of his speech, which could have seemed monotonous but for the character which underlay it; the expression of inspissated gloom; the curious way of looking up at you, which some (from Socratic memory) likened to that of a bull but which was in fact gentler – more reminiscent of a heifer disturbed while softly grazing; and, very occasionally, the passionate outburst of anger, cold and hollow in tone.

All this formed an engaging counterpoint to his warm and amusing personality. He had a strong sense of the absurd, and could mock himself readily. There was ripe laughter at his own jokes and those of others ('t ...t ...t ...' was the sound it usually made). He had what one novelist has described as an instinct for the irresponsible playfulness of conversation. During such conversation, his pipe would be endlessly lit, and the smoke of quiet contentment would curl up to the ceiling. Here was company which not only entertained you but also created the strong feeling that, beneath the frivolity, you had someone of weight on your side.

Gaiety and high spirits were yet more in evidence when he had escaped from his cares to Scotland. I recall James Duff, who when south of the border was an even soberer citizen than Walter, producing a slightly risqué limerick as we walked on the hills above Loch Duich. It was not sufficient to give an appreciative smile: Walter felt that we must render this great work into idiomatic Greek elegiacs, and then chant both versions lustily into the teeth of the wind. Later, with Jane and the family, Mull was the place for shedding cares and giving oneself over to simple fun. Walter might be Rugby's Headmaster or Magdalene's Master in the south, but here the happy and venturesome child, whom everyone needs to let out of prison when on holiday, could have full scope.

One secret of his success with boys was the way in which he would put himself in their care, particularly in College at Eton. The word would go round, 'Walter's low; what are we going to do about it?' Quite often human pyramids would then be built, *Delina Delaney* would be read aloud until the reader collapsed in laughter, or particular songs would be tunelessly sung. Walter would be cheerful again (the whole thing was for our benefit as well as for his); his eye would lower with that soft, conspiratorial look and the bark of laughter would break out. I suspect that the appeal of Socrates to the young was very similar: he too probably caused them to grow, in character as in intelligence, by disarming them with trust and equality, by making even the dimmest of those around feel that they had something to give and that their tutor was a kind of personal possession. Subsequently, when he was a headmaster and had a charming young wife and family, Walter had no need to share himself out in this way. But the readiness to be vulnerable and dependent on others continued to be part of his charm.

In fact, he had considerable self-confidence. Only so could he do, without worrying, things that he wasn't very good at, like singing or games, and take grim delight in his own lack of skill. He was certainly, like Bishop Ullathorne, very strong on humility. A story told about one headmaster of Shrewsbury always brings Walter to mind: taking parents round the school, he threw open the door of a classroom and found, written on the blackboard, the words 'The headmaster is an old fool'. Unabashed, he turned to the parents and said, 'The melancholy truth stares me in the face'. Some of us can only hear the words in Walter's tone of voice. But, in serious matters, he minded very much what people thought of him, and he was quite as sensitive to slights as most of us are. I am ashamed that, though he caused me to be co-opted on to the Rugby Governing Body shortly before he left, I had to miss the unhappy final meeting of which James Hunt writes. Walter's distress is easily understood.

He has been described as a conservative. I should say rather that he was a traditionalist, knowing how much he himself owed to others who had vision from the past and a deep respect for earlier wisdom. Auberon Waugh, in a review, described the world of public school headmasters as 'an area of English society which still flourishes away from the limelight – self-contained, modest, high-principled, and rather pleased with itself'. This is fair comment. But, within that circle of men who were in the main content to change things only gradually, Walter was not one for dying in the last ditch. He made plenty of changes where he saw they were needed; and he had the liberal approach and the impatience with flummery and pomposity that I like to think characterise all intelligent men.

He read widely and had an exceptionally good memory for other people's apophthegms; for he was very ready to be (in the distorted words of the prayer) 'needful of the minds of others'. So he often appropriated the best of what he encountered. But his quick wit and happy turn of phrase also enabled him to coin memorable remarks of his own. As a result, he was one of the few schoolmasters (George Turner was another) who had his comments eagerly collected by colleagues and pupils, later to be recalled with affection.

Yet it was Walter's distinctive and unusual personality that made him truly memorable. The Johnsonian 'bottom of good sense' was topped by contrasting colours grave and gay. This introduction has not done full justice to his range of qualities, lovable oxymoron that he was. But I hope it has whetted the appetite for the full meal which lies ahead for the reader; for there are many who recall Walter Hamilton with a very special delight and remain grateful for having sported in his shade.

THE EARLY YEARS

Donald Wright

WALTER SPOKE LITTLE of his forebears and was reticent about his childhood and school. From the age of eleven he was to win his way from one world into others. It was a progress that gained spectacular momentum, surprising him at each stage until middle life. Such was the rapidity and distinction of his academic achievements that one only caught from him flashes of pride in his upbringing or, unremarkably in the circumstances, a parading of what he used characteristically, if immodestly, to call his humble origins. They could have been far worse!

Walter's grandfather, son of William Edward Hamilton who had had a rope-making business in Scotland, was born in 1841, and his father, Walter George in 1875. His grandfather, called George Miles Edward, became a teacher of distinction. Having qualified at Highbury Training College, he taught first at St John's School, Hoxton, and then at Holy Trinity, Rotherhithe. In 1867 he married another teacher, Annie Smale, daughter of a London lawyer; and in that year, aged twenty-six, he obtained his first headship. Two years later he moved to become head of Langbourn Ward Schools, and when in 1874 these were amalgamated with the Cornhill and Lime Street Ward Schools, George became head of the former and Annie of the latter.

Meanwhile, he had been on the executive of the NUT since its inception, and long before it received recognition

George was earning a reputation as a 'strong, wise and energetic' worker, and an 'expert in finance over a wide field'. He became treasurer of the union in due course and on his retirement in 1916 he was made an honorary member. When, after the War, new offices were built, Hamilton House was named after him, 'serving as a reminder of his splendid service'. He had given thirty-two years to the cause, during which union membership increased from 12,000 to 94,000. George Hamilton was also made a Fellow of the Educational Institute of Scotland. He was a devoted Freemason, becoming Deputy Provincial Grand Rank and Grand Swordbearer, 'with a record of honour of which any man might well be proud'.

Walter (George) was therefore the child of a single-minded teacher and a successful man of the world. He was not the first, or the last, to have such a father who was overbearing. Born in the year when his parents became joint-heads, Walter G. was brought up strictly and to do what he was told. He was put to work in the City as a young man, and by the turn of the century, aged twenty-five, he was earning a modest wage as a mercantile clerk in the tea trade. Then, in 1905, he married Caroline Mary Stiff. She was a schoolmistress five years older than himself, whose father was employed abroad in the Colonies. Three years later, on 10 February 1908, Walter was born. He was to be Catford born and bred. In those days the neighbourhood was an outer London suburb on the edge of the country.

Walter G., who had been well schooled, was a relaxed man, rather slightly built, and one of uncomplicated goodwill who mixed easily. He went about life affably without complaint and with an eye for practicalities. Caroline was tall and clever, somewhat humourless and daunting to meet, and not as outgoing. She could be difficult in fact. She was however well-read, had a very active mind, and, like the Victorian she was, knew the value of a good, well-grounded education. If Walter G. could have had his life over again he used to say he might have become an engineer. And if Walter's mother had been born half a century later she might have gone to Oxford or Cambridge. Soon after they were married, they moved to a newly built terrace house, 121 Broadfield Road, one of hundreds on the Corbett Estate. A. C. Corbett Esq., MP was a property developer in a very big way even by today's standards. He was putting up houses in that area on a huge scale, with wide roads to provide good access. No. 121 had been put up for sale, on a 999-year lease at £585. So it was substantially built and well appointed. Broadfield Road, like other roads parallel and at right-angles to it, is a long one, with similar houses on both sides. By today's standards the houses make a modern church vicarage look shoddy. When Walter was born, his parents decided to employ a general factotum. Her name was Ella McCarthy, and she remained with them for the rest of their lives. She therefore had much to do with Walter in his early years, caring for him when necessary and answering to the family's needs. She used to tell of the time when, aged four, he absent-mindedly walked backwards (not for the last time) off a pier on the south coast when they were on holiday; and of how he would spend hours before going to school cleaning his shoes on a piece of newspaper because he would read it at the same time.

No. 121, then, was to be home for Walter for nearly the first twenty-five years of his life. There were four bedrooms, two rooms downstairs, a store room, and a kitchen. The ceilings were high and much of the furniture built-in. The garden was small. The house still stands where it did, although the four adjoining on one side were destroyed with many fatalities by a land-mine in 1941 and were rebuilt after the war. Walter's parents would have been maimed, if not killed, had they remained there. But they moved in 1932 to 89 Inchmery Road, nearer the centre of Catford and about a mile west, and in what was considered the better part. By then, Walter G., having made his way, had become a merchandiser in the grocery trade, including tea, and was considerably better off even if he never really enjoyed the work.

Walter had a narrow closed-in start to life. He was very well cared for, but isolated from the company and pleasures of other children. However, later on and as he looked back, he did not feel that his parents had been over-possessive, despite the anxiety for him his mother could not help betraying. It was to prove understandable. A new school, free, and the latest of its kind was opened in 1904 in Brownhill Road, now a part of the South Circular, not more than half a mile away. This was Catford Central School for infants, girls and boys (each with separate entrances and departments) up to the age of twelve, and for boys only after that. Spike Milligan went there. But for Caroline Hamilton there was only one way to educate her young son: she would undertake it herself, and she did so assiduously during those years, until he was nine. Nearly all Walter's knowledge of other people came from the books he read. With his mother's encouragement he found his voracious appetite for them, and round the corner in Sandhurst Road was, and still is, the small but very good lending library which, later on, he was to pass four times a day as he walked twice to and from school. When his father's leave permitted they took Walter to Scotland (the Trossachs quite often), and he never forgot the first time he saw Edinburgh Castle from a visit they paid when he was four. He was always to be proud of his Scottish seed.

However he never felt he knew his father well. From the age of six and until he was ten he never saw him at all, for with the outbreak of war in 1914 Walter G. volunteered for service with the Kitchener armies in France. He did not return home until after the armistice. At least he had come through; but his absence emphasized the loneliness of mother and son at home, even if Walter's presence in the house helped to take her mind off the casualty lists to some extent. In 1917 Caroline decided he should go to a day preparatory school, called Malvern House, in Lewisham Park, but it turned out to be a very disappointing one.

Then Walter G. came home from the war and in the following year Walter was old enough to try for the local grammar school, later renamed St Dunstan's. His entry depended on his winning a scholarship from the Governors. He won one, tenable for 'school-life' and as a day-boy. His parents were also awarded a bursary from the newly subscribed Kitchener Fund, the first mention of an association which was to benefit Walter again; and which he in turn was to assist years later, first as a selector for its awards, and eventually as a trustee of the Fund itself. He could not have gone to St Dunstan's without financial assistance.

Thus began, after a diffident start, an outstanding school career. The school's *Chronicle* records it as follows:

W. Hamilton – Prefect since September 1924; Captain of Wilson House; Sergeant in the Corps.; Cert. A. 1926; Second XV Rugger 1925; Second Colours 'Crosse and Captain of the Second XII 1926; Editor of the 'Chronicle'; Secretary of the Debating Society; Matriculated 1923; Higher Certificate 1925; State Scholar; Kitchener Scholar, Classical Scholar, Trinity College, Cambridge.

Seldom has there been a member of the School who has had so great a success in so many activities. He played games with a fair measure of ability, edited the 'Chronicle' for two years, and was the mainstay of the Debating Society; yet all this is overshadowed by his remarkable scholastic success.

He leaves us to take up a Classical Scholarship at Cambridge, where we are sure he will prove a worthy successor to E. C. Prussia.[1]

---

[1] E. C. Prussia changed his name to Yorke following the outbreak of war in 1914: he was a Mods Don at New College, Oxford, for 40 years.

This end-of-year summary of his time at school seeks to show Walter's success as the most versatile and auspicious in its end-of-year list of leavers. One would scarcely appreciate just how promising from his own account of those years:

I was at St Dunstan's from 1919 to 1926 ... I am sure my parents' object in sending me there was to get me the best education locally available. They could not have done better ...

I was a very shy and timid boy, totally lacking in self-confidence. I lived about a mile [more like two I reckon, Ed.] from the school and walked there and back twice a day.

I was greatly in awe of anybody in authority, whether masters or boys, and although I was keen to make friends I did not really know how to set about it. There was a certain amount of what I now see was very mild bullying, but by modern standards discipline was strict. The headmaster was C. M. Stuart, who had been there for thirty years, a remote and terrifying figure, with whom I cannot recall any personal contact ...

My first form master was an amicable man called E. J. Smith, but the next, whose name was Rice, was a surly creature who kept us standing in a semi-circle round him for much of the time and changing places as we succeeded or failed in answering his questions. Other masters I clearly remember were Tomkins, a red-faced man of stormy temper who had a probably undeserved reputation among the boys for drink, and a totally ineffective chemist whose name I have forgotten. I remember him because he was foolish enough to bring me out top in chemistry just before I took the School Certificate. On the strength of this I was awarded a prize. A few weeks afterwards it was revealed that I had obtained 13 per cent in the certificate examination.

The master to whom I owe a really overwhelming debt, and who may truly be said to have determined the whole course of my life was R. S. Bate.[2] He was an admirable scholar by any standard, and he divined possibilities in me of which I was quite unaware. When I took the School Certificate in 1923 he told me

---

[2]R.S.B. ensured that Walter sat for the Trinity scholarship, and not for Pembroke's which had first been considered.

Six years later, when Walter was a Prize Fellow at Trinity, Bate wrote to him asking him to become his executor. In his will he left him some of his classical books.

and my parents that if I were prepared to work really hard he thought I could get a classical scholarship to Cambridge. This in spite of the fact that I knew no Greek, which was not taught below the VIth form.

I *did* work hard, and in seven terms I won a major scholarship in Classics at Trinity, Cambridge. When I look back I really cannot imagine how R. S. Bate managed it. Without him I should probably not have gone to a university at all. He taught me and, I think, two others in a small room called Room Y at the end of the bottom corridor. The time he spent on us must have represented a very lavish use of manpower, but over the years he produced several good classical scholars besides myself, notably E. C. Prussia (afterwards Yorke), a Fellow of New College, and C. C. Alberry, who became a noted Coptic scholar and was killed in the second war. No school in the country could have had a more talented and successful teacher of the Classics.

In my time the school's activities were much more exclusively confined to work than they are now. I don't remember that there were any communal meals. I walked to school and like many others I went home to lunch, and I suppose those who didn't brought sandwiches. I don't recall anything much in the way of societies, though the present system of houses existed for games. I was in Wilson. I was no real good at games – hopeless at cricket, mediocre at Rugger, a bit better at lacrosse. In my last year I was captain of the 2nd lacrosse team, which won the South of England competition. I was a sergeant in the Corps and went to two annual camps at Tidworth, at one of which I was tossed in a blanket. I greatly envied successful athletes and would have given anything to be like them. Ten years later, however, it gave me great pleasure to hear the wife of the farmer, in whose field the Eton scouts were camping also, say of me, 'That Mr Hamilton though no doubt a very athletic gentleman, needs a lot of honey to sweeten his disposition'.

There was a more relaxed atmosphere after F. G. Forder became headmaster about half way through my time. As I rose through the school I saw something of him, but we were not really congenial to one another. I was a prefect, although I cannot remember what powers or privileges this conferred. I do recall, however, a conversation with the headmaster in which he told me he was not going to appoint me head of the school. I took this hard, but I expect that he was quite right as I was still excessively shy and immature socially. The boy he did appoint was Stephen Usherwood, who was (and remained) one of my few close friends. I remember that in his absence I had to deputise for him at the OD dinner and make a speech, the first speech I ever made. I have no idea what I said, but I remember being absolutely terrified.

To Walter's own account of his days at school can be added a little more colour. A contemporary, whose home was on his way to school, often saw him passing by: 'To a brat in Form 1 a prefect was someone to stand in awe of,' he recalls, 'but Hamilton stood out to us little boys as he sported a very short haircut – over the whole of his head, such that he was known to us as Convict 99 . . . A few years later, at a prefects' concert, he and another senior boy, who also read the lesson on the last day of that school year dressed in officer cadet uniform, belted and with a very large sword, sang a song called "Bible Stories". It brought the house down together with the wrath of the Headmaster, F. G. Forder. The other boy, whose name was Frank Price, was dressed in "Empire Outpost" tradition: topee, Sam Browne, khaki shirt, and long shorts, puttees and brown boots. He carried a large pair of pincers with which he periodically extracted Hamilton's teeth – pieces of chalk. Hamilton was dressed loosely (but sartorially) as a very devout but not very "with it" parson.'

Walter was never to forget what he owed to St Dunstan's. He was grateful to it for the rest of his life, and proud of it. Once he concluded an argument with Richard Crossman about the public schools by exclaiming, 'The difference between you and me, Crossman, is that you went to Winchester and I went to a grammar school.' He became a Governor in 1966 and remained one until his death. He was Deputy Chairman for all but six of the twenty-two years, playing a key role in the decisions of the Board. The

Headmaster today, Brian Dance, recalls the stage in so many meetings when the Chairman turned to Walter ('as he invariably did'), asking 'And what does Dr Hamilton think?' Walter was sitting there with pipe in mouth, eyes twinkling over his half-glasses, apparently no more than partly attentive, only to remove the pipe to say 'I think we should support the Headmaster', or words to that effect.

Whilst he was Master of Magdalene he was regularly a generous and congenial host at the annual Cambridge dinner of Old Dunstonians in residence. 'His benign and often quizzical attitude to the undergraduates', writes the Headmaster, 'almost gave credibility to the story that he used to address Magdalene freshmen, saying, "At Magdalene, gentlemen, we have no rules, and if you break them you will undoubtedly be sent down."'

2

TRINITY

W. H.: Undergraduate 1926–29; Prize Fellow 1929–31;
Fellow 1931–35; Assistant Lecturer, Manchester 1931–32

John Morrison

WALTER CAME UP to Trinity from St Dunstan's Grammar School in October 1926 with a major scholarship in Classics. As an undergraduate he was judged a loner, but he succeeded in making some close friends. Guy Furnivall, who was a year senior to him at Trinity (and taught me ancient history at Charterhouse on going down) knew him and says: 'His simple direct and rather mournful manner had a peculiar appeal. I fancy he always remained deeply modest.' The mournful manner and the modesty were often not quite serious. Guy reports a remark: 'I don't know what is the matter with me, Furnivall, but I always seem to get everything *right.*' The story brings back vividly the tone of voice and the short resonant laugh which followed. Others of his Trinity friends at this time were Anthony Martineau and Denys Wilkinson. He and Denys Wilkinson were both in the first class in Part I of the Classical Tripos at the end of their first year (Walter having won a Craven University Scholarship in the meantime). First classes qualified them both for a bursary to travel to Greece. They went together the following Easter. Walter was a Chancellor's Classical Medallist in 1928, won the Porson Prize for a Greek verse composition in March 1929, and in Part II of the Tripos in the following June was placed in the first class with distinctions both in the whole examination and in ancient philosophy, thus concluding an undergraduate career in which he could hardly have done better.

Nick Hammond (subsequently Tutor of Clare, Headmaster of Clifton and Professor of Ancient History at Bristol) speaks of taking an examination with him (possibly Part I of the Tripos or one of the examinations for University Scholarships). Nick with his usual cheerfulness and ebullience said as he went out what an easy piece of translation or composition had been set, while Walter, who was subsequently known to have come out top of the candidates, complained in his gloomiest tones of how 'frightful' it had been.

Patrick Duff, a Fellow and Roman lawyer, returned from America in 1927 and got to know Walter as a friend of Anthony Martineau, whose brother, Richard Martineau, he had known for some years. He speaks of him as 'a very interesting person from early days with a well-stocked memory, witty and very amusing'. Add these qualities to Guy Furnivall's description and the result is probably a fair picture of Walter as an undergraduate, as indeed it is of the man I saw when I came up to Trinity as an undergraduate in 1932.

Harry Sandbach, who had been holding a lectureship at Manchester University, came back to Trinity as a college lecturer in 1928 and was Walter's Director of Studies in ancient philosophy for Part II of the Tripos. Harry said that he 'saw something of Walter when he started research after the Tripos, and set him off on a subject in Plutarch on which he himself in fact was doing some work at the time (*Classical Quarterly*, xxiii, pp. 15–16). He was hoping very much that Walter 'would continue in research, expanding on the subject he had given him. Plutarch today (1990) is popular. In those days not so: he was thought of as a boring old writer.'

It was in the two years after his very successful undergraduate career that he began to widen his circle of friends in College. Patrick Duff, Richard Martineau and Walter went abroad together. Through the Martineaus he

11

became a member of the Trinity Lake Hunt[1]. He was also invited to teach Greek and Latin composition to Trinity undergraduates, including Enoch Powell who came up in 1930 from King Edward's School, Birmingham. His description of Walter in this connection is particularly apt. 'I came to know, which was the start of greatly liking and respecting, Walter Hamilton when he was a graduate student resident in College at Trinity Cambridge in 1932, and I was invited to submit to him for appraisal my undergraduate pieces of required translation into Latin or Greek. My predominant recollection of him then was his self-deprecatory but armoured modesty of speech and manner. . . . It was an education in itself to watch him wielding this instrument with his characteristic and well-practised drawl; and I rejoiced to find him still in full enjoyment of it at our subsequent all-too-rare chance encounters down the years.' The 'armoured modesty' which he 'enjoyed to the full' and 'the characteristic and well-practised drawl' are traits marvellously well identified and, in monumental phrases, described.

I may perhaps be allowed to balance the account by adding a few sentences from a letter which Walter sent in February 1939 to James Duff, by that time Warden of the Durham Colleges, when asked by him to appraise Enoch Powell for the chair of Greek at Durham (which I subsequently occupied). 'Of the excellence of his scholarship there can be no question and though his standards may seem pedantically austere and exalted, I think that severe intellectual discipline of the kind that he would offer is a far better thing for a university than the vague enthusiasm so common nowadays. As a scholar I really think that he is in the Housman tradition and that he would add distinction to any chair that he occupied. It is a pity that he carries reverence for Housman so far as to imitate him both as a controversialist and a

---

[1]The Lake Hunt is referred to in some detail on pp. 19 and 90.

poet.... He himself would deny this conscious imitation, but it is difficult to escape the conviction that it has considerable influence on his behaviour. His insatiable ambition saves him from adopting the habits of a recluse.... He is arrogant and his manner is at first unpleasing, but he is less impervious to the softer influences than he appears to be. It is however true that ambition is his guiding motive.' This brilliant, if artificial, tourney where Walter plays Gibbon to Enoch Powell's Thucydides reveals nearly as much in each case of the describer as of the described.

In October 1931 Walter submitted a dissertation for a research Fellowship at Trinity, and was elected. Anthony Blunt, who competed unsuccessfully the same year, sent Walter a telegram:

> O blest Communion, Fellowship divine,
> We feebly struggle, they in glory shine,
> Yet all are one in thee, for all are thine.

When Blunt himself was successful the following year there is no evidence that Walter replied with the line from the same hymn, 'But lo! There breaks a yet more glorious day'.

Walter's dissertation concerned Plutarch's essay in the *Moralia* on *The Face which appears in the Orb of the Moon*, a title which, he remarked once, 'seems to provide more amusement than the work in fact supplies'. He subsequently published the gist of parts of it in the *Classical Quarterly*, xxviii (1934) pp. 24–30, 175–82. (The same volume of the *CQ* contained (pp. 159–74) an article *Studies on the Greek Reflexive – Thucydides* by Enoch Powell which he must have written as an undergraduate.) Harry Sandbach was one of Walter's referees and remembers that another of the referees commented that it was very remarkable that Walter had dealt in an understanding way with the *actual* words used by Plutarch. Harry said, in general, that Walter was a clever man, with his feet very much on the ground. He had hoped that he would widen his knowledge of the period he started on and thought him capable of making his mark in the general knowledge of the period. He had made a very promising beginning.

The work which Walter did on the myths contained in three of Plutarch's writings was concerned to demonstrate the close connection between those myths and the myths of Plato, both about the fate of the soul after death. Walter was much influenced by the most remarkable, and inspiring, of the classical scholars in Cambridge at the time, Francis Cornford, who was also a Fellow of Trinity. He learned from him the breadth of intellectual attitude and the completely un-arrogant confidence ('armoured modesty') with which he approached the relevant texts of Plutarch and Plato in the belief that they, rather than the scholars who had written about them, would produce answers to the questions he wanted to ask. He read the authorities, of course, but gave to them no greater respect than he did to his own scholarship. The published papers are available for reading and are too esoteric for quotation here. In two or three places indication is given of his plans for future work in his adopted field. One section of the dissertation shows an interesting aspect of his mind:

'[Plutarch's] faith in divine revelations renders it unlikely that he did not take stories such as that of Timarchus [in the *de genio Socratis*, and Thespesius in the *de sera numinis vindicta*] at their face value. Indeed it is even possible that belief in such visions was supported by actual psychical experiences, taking much the same form as they do now.' Francis Cornford had drawn his attention to such an experience (of a man called Wiltse) related by F. W. H. Myers [*Human Personality* II, pp. 315ff] 'which presents such striking points of resemblance to the stories of Timarchus and Thespesius that it cannot be passed over in this connection'. He summarises Wiltse's and Timarchus' stories, and the resemblances *are* very remarkable. He concludes: 'I am not competent to draw any conclusion from this comparison, or

14

to criticise the testimony quoted by Myers; all that I am concerned to point out is that, if the claims of those who say that they have experienced such states in our own times are well founded, the possibility must not be excluded that Plutarch may be drawing to some extent on the actual experience either of himself or of others, and that the imagery common to both the ancient and modern instances may be inherent in the minds of all who are capable of such experiences. This, however, is a question which must be left to the psychologist.' Subsequently this passage from his dissertation was used to conclude a paper presented to an audience. The sentence was added: 'Alternatively, Wiltse may have been recently reading Plutarch.'

There is a paper in Walter's handwriting which Donald Wright has sent me. It is undated and appears to be a discourse on philosophy in general. Two or three pages, the first two and the last qualify, I think, for inclusion here:

Philosophy in its broadest sense, the desire to find out the truth about the universe and ourselves, is a hopeless quest. In Europe it has been at work for over 2,500 years and has attracted to its service some of the best minds in all times and countries; in proportion as man became more civilised, so he became more speculative, but no system has ever yet commanded more than a very partial assent or brought man much nearer to an answer to the question which God addressed to Job out of the whirlwind: 'Where wast thou when I laid the foundation of the earth?' I stress this necessary incompleteness or defect in philosophy at the outset, not because I regard philosophy as a subject unworthy of serious study – quite the contrary – but it is only in so far as we grasp the fact that any philosophical system is nothing more than the attempt of a single finite mind to grasp the nature of a reality, of which it is itself but an infinitesimal part that we can understand, and not be put off by the existence of philosophies of widely different types. However firm a philosopher's resolve may be to follow the argument wherever it may lead him he cannot escape either from his own temperament or from the mental character of his age, and both will influence his system just as his system, if it is strong and vital enough, will help in time to form the mental climate for his successors. There are fashions in philosophy as there are in hats, and there are also certain types of philosophic attitude which are the products of certain types of temperament. The object of this paper is to furnish some kind of thread or clue, by which these fashions and types in the history of thought may be recognised.

There is, however, a further complication. Philosophy, in so far as it restricts itself to intellectual processes as a means of reaching true conclusions about reality is to be distinguished on the one hand from religion, which requires an emotional as well as an intellectual response, and on the other science, which proceeds by experiment and observation of the sensible world. But, though it is easy enough to draw this distinction in theory, in practice philosophy tends often almost to identify itself, now with religion and now with science. One may, in fact, distinguish two main types of temperament among philosophers according as they incline to find the ultimate in the world of sense or in some super-sensible reality. This distinction is particularly well marked in ancient philosophy, and almost corresponds to the distinction between Aristotelian and Platonist, but it can be traced as well in more modern systems.

Walter then proceeds to look at philosophical study in the light of these preliminary remarks and concludes:

Until the end of the nineteenth century philosophy, or at any rate the study of the views of the great thinkers of the past, was a pursuit which could be followed with profit by any person of intelligence, but now, owing chiefly to the influence of science, philosophy has lost its amateur status and only professionals, of whom I assuredly am not one, can enter the arena. But the fashion like other philosophical fashions will probably pass, and whatever the activities of mathematical or logical philosophers may be, nothing, as far as I can see, will stop the ordinary man who has a taste for such things from speculating on the nature of his own and the world's existence, as best he may. There is an instinct to do it which appears to be innate, or as Kant would say, a priori; it is a part of the equipment with which we come

Walter, 1910, not quite three years old.   *Aged about 19.*

Lake Hunt 1933. Standing: Walter, extreme left; fifth to the right of him Kitson Clark, then Outram Evennett, David McKenna, and far right John Morrison. Seated, middle row: Patrick Duff on the extreme left; two from him Adrian and then Charles Crawley. Sitting on the ground: Alan Hodgkin, centre, and on the right Malcolm Robertson.

Above: *Filling sandbags at Eton, probably
1939. Walter facing the camera, left foreground.*

Left: *Teaching behind the octagonal table at
Eton, 1933.*

Below: *Eton, about 1946.*

into the world. 'All men', says Aristotle at the beginning of the *Metaphysics* 'desire to know'; and if this utterly inadequate paper has contributed in the slightest degree to the satisfaction of that desire in anybody, it will have surpassed the expectations of its author.

Before he had submitted his dissertation at Trinity, Walter had accepted a lectureship at Manchester for one year. There he fell under the spell of James Duff, Patrick's elder brother, whom he already knew, and who now held the chair of Education in that university. He was to form a close friendship with him. At the end of his year (June 1932) they both appear in photographs taken at the Trinity Lake Hunt. Their wartime correspondence is given in a subsequent chapter.

Walter returned to Trinity to take up his research Fellowship in the autumn of 1932. Coming up as a freshman for the Michaelmas Term I was a member of a class of undergraduates taking Part I of the Classical Tripos which met weekly in Walter's rooms on E staircase in Great Court. On the first occasion I found myself at the wrong end of King's Parade without a gown when I should have been entering Great Court. I arrived breathless and gownless and was unable to conceal my confusion because Walter assigned me the front chair. I was not late again.

Of Walter as a young Fellow Patrick Duff said: 'He did not *shine* and (in that respect) was very unlike an Oxford don. He hadn't got a hard edge, but he had natural gifts and worked hard.' David Graham-Campbell, who was to become Headmaster of Glenalmond and before that a Housemaster at Eton, was an undergraduate of Trinity in his second year in 1932 and had rooms on the same staircase in Whewell's Court as I did. (My rooms had the advantage that if I looked out of my window at the right moment I could see Housman shaving in the window of his rooms over the gate to Sidney Street.) David writes of his friendship with Walter:

If it was not John Graham (later to be the Superior at Mirfield) that brought us together it would have been either Michael Gresford-Jones, the widely beloved Chaplain in those days (later Bishop of St Albans), or possibly Patrick Duff. One thing that all had in common was that they were amongst those who supported the Chapel services which few young Fellows did.

I guess that Walter found in each of these men the warmth that he craved for. I imagine that he had not found it easy to make friends when he first came up – with his shy and reserved nature and his lack of money – though he *did* make friends, in particular Denys Wilkinson who went on to precede him as a Classics master at Eton. Walter was not impressed by the richer undergraduates, too many of whom came to Trinity from Eton; and he used to hold forth about 'the gilded youth' and how different *he* was, until it became a sort of pose, just as the depression, from which he certainly did suffer from time to time, was turned by him into a sort of 'Eeyore' act. I think that one of the things which drew us together was his discovery that not all Etonians were rich – and idle.

He was also terribly sensitive and sometimes quick to sense slights where none was intended. I remember one dinner-party given by Gaillard Lapsley (an elderly and most hospitable History don) to a number of undergraduates, and to Walter and probably another young don. One of the party was Charles Fletcher, a very good-looking Etonian scholar and rowing Blue, and Gaillard was nothing if not an admirer of all such things. At some moment after dinner Gaillard found some excuse to take Charles into the inner sanctum to show him one book or another, conduct which Walter regarded as a slight on the rest of us but on *him* in particular – and for days would not let the matter drop!

Dinner parties of this kind were regularly given by the other bachelor dons – Winstanley, Collingwood, Jim Butler, Outram Evennett. They and the younger bachelor dons such as Patrick Duff, George Kitson Clark, and Michael Gresford-Jones always set aside the hours from 9 p.m. onwards when they would be at home to anyone who cared to call on them uninvited. At Lapsley's one would be given whisky, at Winstanley's beer and at Patrick's tea. What made it so enjoyable was their determination to treat us as adults and friends, and to give us an enjoyable evening. The younger ones also would join us at

18

lunch-time. Someone had started an undergraduate Lunch Club run on inexpensive lines. Every member in turn would entertain in his rooms any others who wished to come and who wrote their names in a book 48 hours in advance – the only rule being that the host must offer only one simple dish. No alcohol was included. I think that less was consumed in those days.

For the more active there was a much older institution – the Lake Hunt. I think this went back to the undergraduate days of G. M. Trevelyan, and certainly he came once when I was attending. Walter came in 1932, and I have a snapshot of him and James Duff asleep, exhausted on a bank, Walter with his mouth wide open. In that and some subsequent years the future Lord Adrian was 'Master' of the Hunt, the senior don taking part. Jim Butler, Charles Crawley, Patrick Duff, John Burnaby, Kitson Clark, and Outram Evennett were regulars, and there was a group of about 15 undergraduates (including that year Charles Fletcher!). We stayed for six days after the end of the Easter term in a farm house in Borrowdale. Each day two members would be dispatched as hares equipped with hunting horns into a traditionally bounded area of Ennerdale. Half an hour later the rest would set out to round them up guided only by the horns, which the hares blew at intervals, when they felt neglected. The next year, 1933, when Robert Rattenbury, Alan Hodgkin and John Morrison went for the first time, Walter was secretary of the Hunt responsible for collecting the party and informing Mrs Honey at the farm house how many were coming.

Another rather similar party was organised each year by Michael Gresford-Jones. It forgathered in December in a Norfolk windmill. Walter was there in 1932 and somehow managed to get there in 1934.

In *The Times* of 20 September 1933, under the heading Eton College, 'W. Hamilton' was among the new assistant masters mentioned for the coming Half. At Trinity, with Andrew Gow, Harry Sandbach and Robert Rattenbury completing the classical staff, Walter had no particular prospects after the termination of his four-year research Fellowship. His friends Denys Wilkinson and Richard

Martineau were at Eton. Yet he had had serious doubts about accepting the offer. David writes: 'Another quality which Walter had, surely, was humility. Possibly in Trinity days it may have been partly lack of confidence, but he retained it to the end, when there was certainly no lack of confidence. This entered into the long searching of mind before he eventually decided to accept the offer to teach at Eton.' He certainly would have consulted, among others, James Duff, who had, like many educationalists, little sympathy with pure research, especially in the classics. Harry Sandbach's hopes for him to become a Plutarch scholar would have weighed little beside James's advice, and probably Walter's own inclinations. His teaching at Manchester and Trinity was hardly preparation for taking on the lively and extremely able boys of the Head Master's Division at Eton. In those days training in teaching was not thought necessary for someone of high, or even modest, academic qualifications at Oxford or Cambridge, who was seeking a post in a public school. I remember that we all thought David G-C himself rather odd for insisting on going to London (on James Duff's advice, he reminds me) for teacher-training. It was, then, for someone of Walter's background a daunting step to take. I admired his courage.

At Trinity his loss was deeply felt among his now wide circle of friends. Outram Evennett, wrote to him from London on the day the appointment was announced:

I suppose it's you in *The Times* today, and seeing the stability of Gow and his minions I suppose you've done right to take your chance elsewhere. I hope you will be happy and successful, and avoid the blacknesses, as far as humans may. For my own part I shall very much regret your departure. I wish it could only be temporary. Try to forget that you have embraced a profession upon which, with the exception of its highest ranks, the contempt of *the* Great Humanist of our times is continually pouring. Your departure is as though someone had run away to sea from a happy home – But seriously there will be an aching void in our society. What dregs of humanity will the Fellowship election wash on to the High Table? And who shall restrain for us the ragings of Clark? Or discourse to us upon the Flight of the Alone to the Alone?

After some domestic details the letter is signed 'your stricken "Pope"' and a P.S. is added 'Alack! Alack! La chasse des Lacs', referring of course to the fact that a new secretary for the Lake Hunt would have to be found. The appointment *was* as it turned out 'temporary': twelve years later, after the war, he returned to Trinity as a tutor and college lecturer, and university lecturer. I took his place in 1950 when he left again, this time to become Headmaster of Westminster. Patrick Duff said that his mother never forgave me for giving up the chair of Greek at Durham to become a mere tutor at Trinity.

During his first Half at Eton, Walter said he needed cheering up and asked Robert Rattenbury and me (both sharing with him a taste for P. G. Wodehouse) to visit him at Eton one Sunday. Robert drove us down and it being a very wet autumn day we spent the morning and early afternoon reading aloud in his lodgings in the High Street, with almost continuous laughter, a whole Wodehouse novel, I forget which. Later it cleared up and we started to walk across Agar's Plough. Before we had gone a few steps Walter stopped and said: 'If you see smoke rising from behind any of the bushes, look the other way. I *don't* want to be involved.' It was a memorable day, and we formed the impression that he had got over the worst part of his translation, and was really rather enjoying himself.

A conversation, probably in January 1934, recorded by David Graham-Campbell is of interest because of subsequent events: 'We were imagining what jobs we would like to end up in if we each achieved our ultimate dream. At that time

Walter had a young pupil at Eton by the name of Neville, heir to Lord Braybrooke who lived in Cornwall not far from Elwynick. The Visitorship of Magdalene (and the right to appoint the Master, or so at any rate we believed) belonged to the current Lord Braybrooke, and Walter declared that being himself a lazy man, he could not think of a more lovely way to end his days than as Master of Magdalene.' Claiming to be lazy was one of Walter's 'things'. I remember him saying that it was one of the qualities he most admired in James Duff! 'Of course he was not really lazy, yet there was an element of truth behind his remark in that he would always prefer a talk with a friend to an hour spent in classical research. And especially if the talk centred round himself; but egocentricity was of the nicest possible sort, *always*. I should perhaps add that this young Neville was killed in the war and was succeeded by a cousin, so there was no possibility of nepotism in the long run!'

What influence did Walter have on my own life? I find it difficult to separate in my mind his influence from the enormous, and at first shattering, impact which Cambridge and Trinity had on me in that first year. I was recruited by Patrick Wilkinson of King's for the Greek play *Oresteia* (February 1933), and given the part of one of the two aged chorus leaders; and that somehow led to my emergence at the top of a winding iron-staircase in the Guildhall as one of two youthful ark-bearers in Handel's *Jephthah* shortly after. I also spent time with the University Rover Scouts, and walked in a Peace Procession a step behind Anthony Blunt at the point where the Christians succeeded the Communists. The competition in Classics in Trinity was fierce; and I had, though I hardly dared admit it to myself at the time, ambitions for an academic career. Walter helped me to 'sort out my priorities', and encouraged me to take the ancient philosophy option in Part II after one year at Part I (thought risky by Andrew Gow). Shipwreck was narrowly avoided, and I had two years for Part II and could go to non-classical lectures as well as Cornford's. This advice certainly determined my academic interests for the rest of my life. I can blame no one but myself for my later preoccupation with triremes.

This influence, at that moment, was crucial for me. But I think more important still was what one might call Walter's intellectual personality, which I have tried to describe and exemplify above, his 'armoured modesty' of thought and expression. It was so different from the self-conscious 'shining' and cold Housmanic arrogance often then to be found in the groves of Academe. This intellectual personality, rather than any learning or teaching, must have made his colleagues in the teaching profession understand, and appreciate, his unique value, particularly in his contacts, e.g. as Master-in-College at Eton, with intellectually ambitious boys at formative moments in their lives.

David Graham-Campbell has hinted at the critical, love-hate, relationship which Walter had with Trinity and Cambridge in that early period. He certainly had it, and I may well have caught it from him, though I don't remember being conscious of it until later.

When Walter was Headmaster of Rugby and I had moved from Trinity to Churchill, I was much involved in the new entrance arrangements for the Colleges caused by membership of UCCA (which a few senior tutors had persuaded the rest to accept). I used to visit Rugby to try out on him and his Second Master, James Hunt, the various entrance arrangements which were being proposed, and both were immensely helpful. This operation brought home to me how much the upper reaches of British education had been distorted by the specialist demands of Oxbridge, made in terms of the scholarship examinations, which had in turn affected the earlier examinations for state scholarships, and the present A levels. Now that an entrance place at a College led, if need justified it, to full financial assistance, the entrance scholarship examinations could, it seemed to me, be dropped (as indeed they have been), and the specialist pressure on schools eased. The harm however was done and has not been erased. Walter disagreed with me strongly on this (and it must be admitted so did practically everyone else at that time); and I think it was then, but it might have been later, that he said: 'John, why do you always want to *change* things? Why not leave them *as they are?*' I should have answered: 'That is the way I was brought up at Trinity,' but instead I reminded him of Adrian's remark in a speech as Master at Commemoration in 1960 which gave me the proudest moment of my life: 'Morrison is leaving us for Churchill: he has changed Trinity – a little.' For Walter in his early days at Trinity, as for me later, love-hate sentiments, as the poet Catullus observed, were all very well; but, suggesting at best ingratitude and at worst betrayal, they were distinctly uncomfortable. '*Quare id faciam fortasse requiris, Nescio, sed fieri sentio et excrucior*'.

There is one last question to answer: what sort of a place was Trinity when Walter was there as an undergraduate, a graduate student and junior Fellow, in the late 1920s and early 1930s? The answer I try to give must be highly subjective. There were some four to five hundred of us from very different backgrounds. The majority came from the public schools and were financed wholly by their families. They followed very different ambitions, from a golf or rowing or cricket Blue, a distinguished and happy place in a difficult world, service to Britain or the world in one or other capacity, teaching, the Churches, answers to the secrets of man and the universe, to political power whether as saviours or destroyers of the existing order. The giants could be recognised at sight, Alan Hodgkin in physiology, Enoch Powell in classics (then), the future politicians, and the Communists. So in the previous century a future Master of

24

Trinity, seeing a freshman coming up the steps of Hall and standing at a loss before plunging into the babel of Hall dinner, exclaimed: 'He must be a poet!' The freshman was Alfred Tennyson.

Walter saw himself on the one hand (David Graham-Campbell says) and the 'idle rich' on the other, but like many of Walter's Johnsonian apophthegms this was surely spoken more than half in jest. The 'reading men', rich or poor, with only a few exceptions tried hard to pretend they were really idle. The rich were not always idle, or the idle rich. Those who, like myself, just managed to get by on scholarships and help from family did their best, and could succeed, in seeming like the rest. And I think this was true of the 'rich' as well. We all enjoyed ourselves immensely, but of course in different ways. There was no ground for envy.

Money did not make much difference to our politics either. The 'Left', near or far, came, with one or two exceptions (Cairncross), from the comfortable upper middle class, Wykehamists or at any rate from the more expensive public schools. Some tried to disguise their background by adopting 'local' accents and clothes, but it made them conspicuous in College. Their company was an education for the rest of us. Having coffee at a left-wing gathering after Hall shortly after the Italian invasion of Abyssinia I listened to their dismay. The Communist line had been strongly anti-war, but now what? The decision was to wait until the new party line was communicated. The *Daily Worker* didn't wait, and staying pacific had to make a public recantation. Perhaps I was naïve to be shocked, believing that only the uneducated left it to others to make up their minds for them.

I don't think that Walter, any more than most of us at that time was a 'political animal'. He took a gloomy view of the world's future, as well he might at that time, saying that he could not contemplate marrying and bringing children into such a world. But this was mere talk probably coloured by an early disappointment. He had been very fond of a girl who took the Classical Tripos with distinction in the same years as he did. But she had married someone else. He was, to the core, a family man, who having been lonely without brothers or sisters, needed to love and to be loved.

The great advantage of a Collegiate university is that undergraduates, and perhaps more importantly dons, are not thrown together (as tends to be the case in the non-Collegiate ones I have experienced) solely with those reading (or teaching) the same subject. The cross-fertilisation of ideas is perhaps what 'university' means. I certainly found it one of the most exciting aspects of my life as an undergraduate, and afterwards as a Fellow, at Trinity. Most of my friends were not in my own 'patch'. I don't remember Walter speaking of this but he must have experienced it; and I feel confident that it formed a part, perhaps only an unconscious part, of what Trinity did for him, from the time when he first stood at a loss, as I think even the most confident of us did, before plunging into that highly exhilarating babel of ideas and personalities. He gained a breadth of intellectual approach which was to stand him in good stead.

3

ETON: 'THE WAY HE SHOULD GO'

W.H.: Assistant Master 1933–34, 1935–37,
Master-in-College 1937–46

Robert Bourne

TOWARDS THE END of March 1933, Walter travelled to Eton, for the first time in his life, as Cambridge examiner for the Newcastle Scholarship. This examination is, or rather was, since its importance is now greatly curtailed, a searching test in Latin, Greek and Divinity for the leading twenty-five or so Classical Specialists at Eton. Standards were high; if the winner were not already a holder of an open scholarship at one or other university, it was generally because he was too young to have sat for one. Whether Walter's assistance was asked for by those at Eton who knew him, or his name was put forward by the university, is immaterial; his distinction made him a most obvious choice.

For the week of the examination he stayed with the Provost, Dr M. R. James; there was nothing unusual in this, for as a bachelor and a former Provost of King's, Monty James, now in his seventieth year, quite often did entertain the Cambridge examiner: he had a large house and enjoyed renewing university gossip. The two seem to have got on remarkably well: Monty James was a great expert on the novels of P. G. Wodehouse, and was delighted to find his young guest a fellow-admirer. 'Mr Hamilton has a good working knowledge of Wodehouse,' he said later. Whether

Walter had by that time developed any of the skill at *The Times* crossword (it had only been going for four years) for which his host was so celebrated is less certain; more so is the apocryphal nature of the story that Monty James completed the crossword 'while his breakfast egg was boiling, and he did not like his eggs hard-boiled'. In later years Walter was described as being 'of international class' – whatever that may mean – as a solver of these puzzles. More important was Walter's discovery that a number of Etonians were not all of the type with braying voices that made so much noise in the courts of Trinity, something he had already guessed from the behaviour of one or two of his friends there – Anthony Martineau and David Graham-Campbell, in particular.

It was, in fact, with the first of these that Walter had been on holiday in Austria the previous August, when the deaths were reported of four Eton masters in a climbing accident in Switzerland. As Walter and their friends were on their way home, they met another master who had hurried out to arrange the return of the dead men's effects. Although disturbing, the incident had no particular significance for Walter, and he soon dismissed it from his mind. But on his return to Trinity he found a letter waiting for him from Claude Elliott, the Head Master-elect of Eton; he was at Jesus, where he had been Senior Tutor, and asked Walter to come and see him with a view to teaching Classics at Eton that very September. The departure of the outgoing Dr Alington to the Deanery of Durham had already weakened the Classical ranks at Eton (like his predecessors, Dr Alington had taught Latin to the Head Master's Division), but *ad hoc* arrangements had been made to fill the gap until the new Head Master – Elliott was not likely to teach them himself, since his subject was Medieval History – should make an appointment. Now two more Classical masters – one, H. F. E. Howson, a fair scholar – must be replaced and time was very short. Three of the four dead, incidentally, were housemasters, two of them well known to the new Head Master who, himself a mountaineer, now had only one close acquaintance in the school.

Walter was not, at first, at all in favour of going to Eton: he regarded the school, as he said himself, 'with a mixture of envy and hostility not unnatural in the product of a south London grammar school', though he had a few Etonian friends and had much enjoyed his visit there in the spring. His Fellowship still had two years to run, he was enjoying the 'lotus-eating existence' which it entailed, and he was expecting to spend his working life as an academic. But 'his elders and betters' advised him to accept; it would be a good idea to have a year away from the 'myopic atmosphere' of Cambridge, and he might find schoolmastering a 'useful second string'. So at any rate wrote Andrew Gow, at the time a don at Trinity and author of – among more scholarly works – that admirable four-page digest of the entire Greek syntax. He had himself gone from Trinity to Eton in not dissimilar circumstances some thirty years before. Three of the paragraphs of his letter to Walter deserve quotation, they are so very apropos:

1. Every newcomer at Eton is liable to be ragged, and some of the ultimately most successful have been ragged almost out of their lives at first. It is an extremely unpleasant experience, but remember that as you find your method and as you cease to be looked on by the boys as a newcomer, it will, if you are worth your salt, die down and stop. There is, of course, a class of schoolmaster with whom it goes on to the end of his time, and if you were to feel yourself one of those (you won't, I am sure) the sooner the time ends the better. But don't conclude that you are on only a year's experience; and contrariwise, if you are never ragged, don't conclude from this that you are necessarily a good schoolmaster.

2. Don't lose your temper more often than you can help, but if you do lose it (now and again it is quite salutary), make quite

certain that is an experience which nobody present will wish to see repeated. I should be inclined to suppose that the worst possible disqualification for a schoolmaster is to be ridiculous rather than alarming when angry.

3. Boredom and disorder in school are most easily produced by the teacher being inaudible, so remember to speak so that everybody can hear. And try to keep your voice lively even when what you are saying is in itself dull, at any rate to yourself. I mention this because your ordinary speaking voice tends to be low, and is very much nearer monotone that most people's.

Seldom can better advice have been offered to the would-be schoolmaster, and Walter kept this letter all his life. Courageously, he accepted the post, on the understanding that he would return to Trinity after the Summer Half to complete his Fellowship, with no further commitment on either side.

His friend, James Duff, also wrote to him: 'This is only a word to salute you on your debut at Eton. My wishes for you are, in order of priority: (1) that you will be such an instant and unbounded success that by the end of the year you will feel no doubt whatever that a schoolmaster you must be, and (2) failing that, and if you feel the slightest doubt about liking the *work*, as distinct from the amenities of life, you will give it up after the year ...

'My best friend at Eton is Arthur Foot; he remains obstinately normal, and is therefore thought very eccentric indeed there. All good wishes. You should at the least have an amusing year.'

The start of a schoolmaster's career is always daunting; for Walter that first Half at Eton must have been doubly so. His appointment had been made so late that, so far from being welcomed into a colony (of which more later), he had to occupy very cramped quarters, in a down-town lodging-house – a place where Robert Birley, who had begun life at Eton in fairly similar circumstances, always claimed he had had to sleep in the bathroom. Walter had one Trinity friend, Denys Wilkinson, already at Eton, who had married another Cambridge friend, Gillian Nairn; he had also met Richard Martineau, Anthony's elder brother, already established as teacher of Greek to the Head Master's Division, as well as other leading Classics. Otherwise he knew nobody, and there was no one to explain the place to him as a newcomer. For the Eton of the 1930s was still very largely staffed by old Etonians, nearly all of whom were former Collegers; there was no Common Room, and the only time the masters ever assembled *en masse* was the daily meeting known as Chambers.

The first of these Masters' Meetings, held on the morning of the day the boys returned, did little to cheer Walter. It was also Claude Elliott's first experience of a Masters' Meeting, and, despite the coolness and skill with which he had repaired the damage of the Alpine disaster, the new Head Master was treated by the senior masters, Walter noticed, with a scant respect which almost amounted to browbeating. He had not been their choice for the post – he was, indeed, like Mr Flaggon at Lanchester, a last-minute compromise: he had neither a ready tongue nor a commanding presence, and he had no more experience of schoolmastering than Walter. He was not, in fact, at all a suitable subject for browbeating, as most discovered later, but at this first meeting, handicapped by deafness in his right ear, he didn't cut a very impressive figure. Walter felt, and must have looked, so doleful that Robert Birley, sitting near by, passed him a note: 'Cheer up; it won't always be as bad as this!'

As a temporary master Walter had no pupils of his own (every boy was assigned to a Classical Master who would be his tutor and have responsibility for his education before School Certificate), but the unfamiliar task of preparing for, and correcting the work of, his school divisions kept him busy enough. He was lucky; he had been allotted A2, the Classical

31

Lower Sixth, as his main division (most new masters started with Fourth Form, even such scholars as Andrew Gow), to whom he taught both Latin and Greek. Most of these were Collegers, but one of the few Oppidans,[1] now a Lord-Lieutenant in the West Country, remembers him vividly. 'Walter Hamilton was obviously very green; he had a pronounced accent and a rather lugubrious voice. We ragged him unmercifully. However, he was so nice and took it in such good part and had so good a sense of humour, that it wasn't long before we felt ashamed and desisted, and I know we ended by liking him immensely.'

Walter soon found that he enjoyed teaching a division of boys rather more than the individual supervision of undergraduates, but he was less fortunate with a middle-school Latin group which made up his programme. Though by no means the toughest elements of the school – he never had to face a really thuggish crew – they resisted his attempts to establish his authority, until one day he imposed on a particular trouble-maker a punishment so severe, or so it seemed, that the culprit went straight back to his house and, after ensuring that his Dame (Matron) was watching, swallowed a considerable amount of Lysol. He was lucky, for not all Dames were trained in nursing. She did the right thing, and his life was saved, but the boy was an inveterate wrongdoer under a 'final warning', this last punishment being too much for him. But from that moment the division gave Walter no more trouble.

As a temporary master without pupils or athletic prowess, Walter was not at first greatly sought after by hostesses of dinner-parties, but his capacity for making friends prevented any feelings of loneliness. Denys and Gillian Wilkinson were already allies; other Classical masters, in particular Richard

---

[1] Members of the school who are not on the foundation and live in a boarding-house outside the College proper.

Martineau and Francis Cruso, a contemporary of Richard's in College at Eton and at Cambridge (a man of many talents, and a very fair scholar) made him welcome; the rest of the Classical staff – some thirty strong – seemed well disposed. Considering that nearly all the Eton masters, except a few Scientists, were ex-public school, that it was an age when social distinctions were still acutely felt, and Walter was reputed to be shy, his ready acceptance was remarkable. 'Someone told me he was so shy,' wrote a Colleger, 'because he was the son of a railway porter at Didcot station. I actually believed it until I read his obituary! Walter was essentially like Melchisedec: no one knew where he came from, and he had no known relations.'

It is clear that authority was also favourably impressed, for soon after his return to Trinity at the end of the Summer Half, Walter received an invitation from Claude Elliott to return to Eton, in September of the following year, 1935, in order to teach Latin to the Head Master's Division. One early pupil even claims that Walter was promised the position of Master-in-College, when it should next be vacant: but although Claude Elliott's judgement of a man's worth was quick and good, and although he had just had a row (and had apologised for it) with Richard Martineau who seemed an obvious choice, so definite a step seems improbable, when there were other possible candidates already well established at Eton. It is more likely that he simply mentioned the possibility of such promotion.

This time Walter did not hesitate for long. He had already decided that he preferred the work of forming boys' minds to that of instructing undergraduates of already moulded character – and life at Trinity was curiously flat. His acceptance was greeted with joy by Richard Martineau and Francis Cruso, both of whom had visited him at Trinity and in the interval had written him long gossipy letters about events at school. In one of these Francis described a

33

celebrated Masters' Meeting where Elliott, at the instigation of several senior housemasters, had refused to consider the possibility of a school play if it meant that boys would appear on the stage dressed as women: should *Macbeth* be put on, then the part of Lady Macbeth must be excised! This astounding victory for the Old Guard, and the Head Master's part in it, led to a feeling of contempt for Elliott among the more liberal young masters.

In another letter Francis begged Walter to come and help him with a troop of Scouts, to the command of whom, much to his alarm, he had unexpectedly succeeded. Their former leader, a master much addicted to horse-racing, had amassed such uncontrollable debts that he vanished from Eton overnight. At that time a young master, unless physically incapacitated, was expected to serve in either the OTC or the Scouts for a few years. So Walter, though never an enthusiastic disciple of Baden-Powell, accepted, since this removed any threat of having to become a make-believe soldier.

An unexpected 'spin-off' from the departure of the 'Welsher' was an invitation to Walter to fill the vacancy thus created at the colony in 2 Weston's Yard. There were some half-dozen of these colonies – largish houses at Eton in which four or five bachelor masters would each have a reasonably spacious study and an adequate bedroom; they took their meals together and employed a cook-housekeeper (and often a daily woman) to look after them. As there was then no Common Room, and most masters arrived as bachelors, such a colony provided an admirable (it was thought an essential) introduction to the complexity of school life. There was much competition for places at the better ones, and their identities were subtly different. Francis was in a notably progressive one, while Richard, who had recently fallen out with the head of a rather old-fashioned establishment, was now ensconced in an artistic milieu.

2 Weston's Yard had an excellent situation and a somewhat conservative reputation, which suited Walter, who was naturally conservative in outlook and felt no very great sympathy with the Arts.

The two principal and most permanent figures in the colony were 'Big Fred' and 'Little Fred' – Fred Coleridge, an old Colleger of great physical presence and athletic ability, and Fred How, a Wykehamist of extreme precision and with a much-imitated drawl: both were very good value and destined to play a major part in Eton life. It was a very social colony; its members dined out frequently and entertained in return, so Walter was plunged quickly into Eton's social life.

Among the leading hostesses (housemasters' wives for the most part, since few others could afford frequent dinner-parties) and certainly the most vivacious and attractive was Grizel Hartley, a corn-gold Nordic beauty of considerable intellect. With cultured interests, and well read, she was now in her mid-thirties and married to a famous Cambridge oarsman, who had taken over Eric Powell's house after the Alpine disaster. Hubert Hartley taught French somewhat erratically, was game for any madcap scheme, provided it was honourable, and was predictable only in his unpredictability. On one occasion he and Grizel were rounding the north-west of Scotland in bad weather in a small sailing-boat and making water fast; a larger vessel, observing their plight, came within hailing distance and offered assistance. Hubert politely declined, calling to Grizel as he did so, 'Bail like hell, but don't let anyone see you doing it.' Near home, Grizel once assisted John Herbert, another rowing Blue and part-inventor of wartime 'Pluto', to drive through Eton in a steam-roller, the top-scoring discovery of an after-dinner treasure hunt; she was still in evening dress, but with the addition, as was apparent when she dismounted, of top-boots.

The Hartleys were most generous hosts; and to be a guest at their dinner-table was always enjoyable. Walter soon succumbed to Grizel's charm, and a friendship developed which only ended with her death over fifty years later. She had no family of her own and she was immense fun. She brought Walter on, gave him confidence, smoothing the rough edges, and helping to make him easier socially. That she should have taken so readily to him may seem surprising, but she was a good judge of character and was quick to appreciate Walter, and a dislike of pretentiousness was something she and he had in common. Certainly he could not bear affectation in others, especially in the form of snobbery. When, later on, a Classical colleague of well-advertised gentility boasted how his pupil room was full of aristocratic names like Cholmondeley and Brudenell-Bruce, Walter countered with 'And mine is full of good old Anglo-Saxon ones like Winch and Snell'.

Life in a colony was rarely cheap; in 2 Weston's Yard it was relatively expensive, but pre-war salaries at Eton were generous, and Walter had an unexpected bit of good fortune. His friends had, during his absence, arranged for his name to be kept (in brackets) on the school list, so that on his return he ranked as a third-year master with a place on the permanent staff and an increase of salary. He even managed to afford an elderly touring-car, registered number AMO 23, which he evidently drove in an erratic manner. Some boys considered he needed their assistance to reverse it out of the garage. Later he acquired another Austin, a majestic 'upright grand' saloon, often seeking reassurance that this model befitted his office.

In return for his salary a Classical Master took pupils besides teaching in school. To build up a pupil room to maximum strength – thirty-six pupils – took some years, but non-classical housemasters were always on the look-out for a promising tutor. Younger pupils would appear daily in Pupil Room for an hour or more doing supervised work, mostly in Latin; older ones, as well as doing Latin exercises (prose or verse) for their tutor, would attend more relaxed seminars, known as 'private business', in his study, generally with an English content. Walter took over the remaining pupils of Jan Crace, a former Master-in-College who had just retired from a boys' house and gone to live in Cornwall, where Walter became in later years a regular visitor.

One of these pupils, already a Classical Specialist, has this to say of his first meeting with Walter. 'My previous tutor was a most kindly man in a formal, old-fashioned way, but I was ready for somebody different. Walter was a breath of fresh air from a world outside. In those days the difference in the way boys, however senior, were looked upon was considerable, and it was delightful to be treated as a person, not just as a boy. But Walter had two safeguards against any abuse of his relaxed style: his personal dignity and his strong principles. You knew where you were with him.' Because of this out-of-school work, most of it in the evenings, a Classical Master taught for comparatively few periods in school.

But his main task was to teach Latin, and often Divinity, to A1, the Head Master's Division, for ten or twelve periods a week (a period in those days lasted fifty minutes). Though Greek was his preferred subject, and that of his research, Walter very rarely taught it to A1, since Richard Martineau had been given that task and, not unnaturally, liked it better – it suited his rapid train of thought and dry humour. But Walter taught exceptionally well too. Naturally slower of speech and more interested in philology, he would insist on a translation better than the obvious, especially when dealing with a stylist like Tacitus; or he would explore the reasons behind a statement.

The main difference was in the two teachers themselves. Richard would sit behind the octagonal table, which served as a desk, wrapped in coat and scarf, and frequently hoarse from cold, pouring out knowledge, as one pupil said, 'like a demi-god', at considerable speed and in no very audible voice. To catch the pearls of wisdom and humour a boy had to listen hard. Walter walked about the room, banging the sleeve of his gown, weighted with chalk or a confiscated squash ball, on bench or table, burying his head in pretended agony at mistakes, rolling his protuberant eyes (as Socrates did) with their large whites until they almost disappeared, using all of an actor's gestures to stimulate interest. He encouraged participation very much more than Richard, but expected it to be at a high level. 'You mortify me, you make me feel positively sick,' he could say in those lugubrious but wryly humorous tones, when a contribution appeared unworthy. He kept, none the less, a conscious distance from camaraderie. When the cares of College in wartime cut into his preparation the monotone noted by Gow sometimes resumed control, and his teaching was thought dull in comparison with Richard's: but Collegers saw and heard far more of Walter, and Richard, until Walter's last year, did not have the burden of a house.

The teaching of A1 was a brilliant double act. 'Its fame attracted aspiring Classical Specialists,' writes one. 'For many of us the prospect was daunting, and the impact devastating. This was learning at a higher level than one had ever dreamed of. But the encouragement was such that one quickly acquired a new attitude: we came to know that scholarship could be fun. Cambridge afterwards was pale by comparison.' And from another, 'Richard and Walter were good foils to each other and between them they showed us the *douceur de vivre*. If the Lycaonians in the Acts had been up to them in the Head Master's Division they would have called Richard Mercury and Walter Jupiter.'

The two of them were largely untrammelled by examination syllabuses – for all the better scholars would be doing Oxbridge papers in December, there was the Newcastle in March, while the Grand July in the summer was partly university-set. Almost any byway could be explored. In one long Michaelmas Half Walter covered just the opening fourteen verses of St John's Gospel, yet the Division was not bored, for his theme – the linking of Greek philosophy to the Christian faith – was of almost as much concern to Walter[2] as it had been to St John.

Walter's success both as a teacher and as a member of the Eton community had not escaped the notice of Hugh Marsden. This extraordinary, gangling, shabby figure, known to all boys as 'Bloody Bill' and to the staff (in politer moments) as H.K. was the one surviving master whom Claude Elliott knew well: they had been exact contemporaries in College. A devoted old Colleger (his father had been the first Colleger to row in the Eight) and a tireless worker for Eton (as he envisaged it), he loved power but shunned its outward manifestations. He was now, largely because so many senior masters had cold-shouldered their new Head Master, Claude Elliott's closest adviser. He saw that the post of Master-in-College would soon be vacant, for John Wilkes, the present incumbent, was rumoured to be courting Alington's daughter, Joan, and known to be a candidate for headmasterships. H.K. wanted the appointment to be a man of his choice.

Master-in-College is, in theory anyhow, a very old title dating back to the sixteenth century, when for the first time the Head Master – who originally filled both roles – appointed a young deputy to College in order to concentrate on his wider duties. The deputy was to be a master in, but not of, College, and his position was still the same in 1862, according to a digest of the Royal Commission's report, which described him as 'an ill-paid young gentleman specially deputed by the Head Master to live familiarly among Collegers and to act as their guide and friend, but not their tutor'. He had no control, of course, over the selection

---

[2]This is plain from the third sermon printed, p. 215, in the appendix and delivered in 1949.

of his scholars, and little power of dismissal; he did not choose the prefects (Sixth Form), and had only a minor part in the choice of his Matron, who looked after the scholars' health and feeding; even a Classical tutor's report on a Colleger was addressed direct to the parents, though by courtesy it was sent to the Master-in-College to read and send on together with his own report. The Master-in-College was normally young, skilled in the Classics, almost always an old Colleger (Alington having been the only exception), and for him to occupy the post for more than eight years was unusual.

The obvious candidate was Richard Martineau; he had been Captain of the School and he had won the Newcastle; he also very much wanted the post. But H.K., when Master-in-College, had formed a poor opinion of Richard's quality as a leader (others probably agreed, though Richard became a much-liked housemaster later on), and was determined he should not get College; and Claude Elliott had no difficulty in accepting H.K.'s view. Francis Cruso was, in H.K.'s eyes, tarred with the same brush (a game leg had inhibited any possible athletic performance, and his liking for music and art did nothing to endear him to H.K., or the Head Master). So H.K. decided to run Fred Coleridge for the post. Fred was, indeed, to become Master-in-College briefly after Walter left, but at the earlier time didn't seem the right choice. Though much the same age as Walter, and a fine games player, he was not an outstanding scholar, and taught only in the lower part of the school; and Claude Elliott, who was never so much dominated by H.K. as popular opinion had it, refused to consider the suggestion. H.K. now turned his thoughts to Walter, and with this idea Claude Elliott, who had a good opinion of Walter, concurred.

On 29 October 1936, Walter wrote to James Duff: 'I dare say you observe that Wilkes has become Warden of Radley. I succeed him at Easter, which was earlier than expected, and I think caused our Head Master some qualms, but he finally offered me the job and I have accepted. So here I am for the next year or two anyway. It all seems very odd, not least the prospect of furnishing a house for oneself . . . I feel a good deal of doubt about having to cope with the complexities of the job, but I am immensely gratified at being offered it.' Duff replied, 'Your letter was most welcome . . . I am really rather glad you are not becoming a Head Master straight away. No doubt you would have done it all right, but you will do it more easily, and with less of a sudden overwhelming extra load, after a few years in College. Christie will do very well at Westminster.'

The appointment was very largely the Head Master's; not even Lord Hugh Cecil, the new Provost (for Monty James had died), was consulted. When the news was released on St Andrew's Day 1936 that John Wilkes was to be the new Warden of Radley, and that Walter was to succeed him as Master-in-College, there was no disapproval and much enthusiasm. He was only the second non-Old Colleger to be appointed. Richard, though it took him some days, wrote him a marvellous letter, in which he did not attempt to hide how much College meant to him, and how greatly he had hoped for the post; but said he knew that under 'the present set-up' he would have no chance, even if Walter were not a runner: so their friendship never suffered the slightest hitch. Denys Wilkinson, it was said, had danced for joy at the news, and congratulations flowed in from Alington, from Jan Crace, from friends at Cambridge and from the Master of Magdalene. He had been at Eton only a little over two years, yet not a single master or old Etonian seems to have objected.

Not all present Collegers, however, were equally delighted. To many Walter was scarcely even a name. One junior – later a figure of importance in the Foreign Office – was at first horrified. He had expected the post to go to one of the several Etonians available and he had hoped for an athlete. Walter he thought of as 'a rather wet academic of obscure origins, with odd mannerisms and an extraordinary voice'. But the favourable reception of the news by the Collegers in A1 soon had College looking forward to his arrival in the Summer Half, 1937.

A Master-in-College occupied a series of rooms in the original building, looking on to School Yard: there were boys' rooms to the side and behind him. The youngest boys were housed in cubicles, or stalls, in Long Chamber: the partitions didn't reach the ceiling, there was barely room for the essential furniture, and real privacy was impossible. The boys were under the control of the Captain of Chamber who dwelt, like Cerberus, at the door; he had considerable powers of punishment, notably a siphon, or length of stout rubber-hose, and was not always restrained in its use. The remaining scholars were mostly in the new buildings facing Weston's Yard, where the most senior had a spacious Common Room called College Reading Room. Beyond this the Matron-in-College and her assistant had their quarters which included the sick-rooms.

The Matron, who was a key figure, on Walter's arrival was Miss George. However, she was soon succeeded by Miss Iredale-Smith, and her appointment would have been largely his. With a kind heart, well concealed by a prickly, formidable manner, she was soon known as 'the Airedale'. Walter admired her efficiency and thought her extremely good at her job. Her responsibilities included the College kitchens and hall, and thus also the entertainments given by the Provost and Fellows. The relationship was always one of employer and employee and she remained a bit frightened of him. It was some time before he found her congenial. A colleague, later Headmaster of Charterhouse, visiting him when ill, was implored, 'For God's sake keep that woman out'. But the boys appreciated her underlying interest, her organisation, and strength of mind. Once when, in wartime, fish was delivered from Harwich by rail, she sent it back as unfit. It was also reputed that College was kept in eggs (which she put down in waterglass in the basement) from a farm she owned in Wales, the scraps being sent there by courtesy of the GWR. But no one knew what befell the hens in the school holidays. The boys, many of them, kept in touch with Miss Iredale-Smith in her retirement and her obituary in *The Times* was written by the then Home Secretary, a fine tribute to a memorable and devoted character.

Though he normally took other meals in his own rooms, the Master-in-College presided over Boys' Dinner in College Hall; but unlike a housemaster, who sat surrounded by his boys, the Master-in-College was, by tradition, seated at the High Table out of earshot of anything they might say. Here Walter was to be joined on most days by two other figures, neither of whom could be described as delightful company. One was the Conduct of Chapel, the Revd Bernard Harvey, who, as headmaster of the Choir School had the right to lunch in College Hall, and is best described as an elderly clergyman of startling dullness. Walter found him irritating and boring. Harvey's sole duty affecting the life of the school was to take the services in Chapel.

The second was a very different person. As Lord Hugh Cecil, the Provost – ennobled in 1942 as Lord Quickswood – had been a witheringly effective speaker in the House of Commons, and a close ally of the young Winston Churchill. Dubbed Lord Hugo Sizzle by comic writers, he had represented Oxford University in the House of Commons for many years. He was an expert in high ecclesiastical affairs and had quarrelled with most, if not all, senior Church dignitaries. Now in his late sixties and in precarious health (he had pernicious anaemia, if mildly), he had quitted politics and, to the general amazement, had been made Provost of Eton – a school he had not liked as a boy and rarely visited since. He had never had a house or servants of his own, so his family, aided by Universal Aunts, equipped the Lodge for him and found the necessary staff – in particular a butler named Tucker, who achieved some notoriety. Quickswood, frail in physique, with restless mannerisms and a high-pitched voice, entertained often and in style at the Lodge. For dinner, tails were obligatory (though boys could get away with dinner-jackets); he wore silk knee-breeches himself. As well as the staff he would invite senior boys, who sometimes repaid his kindness by asking him questions just as he raised his spoon (he ate only soft foods) to his lips. With his natural good manners he held the spoon in his shaking hand until he had given a copious answer: by then the spoon was empty. The game could be played until the butler intervened. Tucker took it on himself to keep the boys, or those he approved of, well supplied with claret and port. Sometimes he simply poured these through their fingers. He was no Jeeves, but in Jeeves's phrase, he was 'keenly alive to the existence of class distinctions'. More than once the boys returned to their houses late and noticeably merry. On one such occasion Walter stoutly tackled the Provost about his flagrant breach of school rules, and elicited a far from generous apology – written, typically, in pencil.

But Quickswood was a witty speaker and enjoyed an argument. Walter, though he might in private refer to the Provost as 'that interfering old fool', and sometimes complain that though he always had a bottle of claret for lunch (and a decanter of gin, well watered and purely medicinal) without ever offering him a glass,[3] found pleasure in crossing swords with him at High Table. For when the Provost read the lesson in Chapel from behind his green eye-shield he would preface the passage with a highly idiosyncratic exposition on its appropriateness: being a Cecil

---

[3]Quickswood would have found it inconceivable to offer one, except to a guest: he lunched at 'home' in London, dined very occasionally, and in the Commons *never* went to the bar – where people *did* treat others. 'Gentlemen' of his standing did not encounter those who could not afford to buy their own, if they wanted it. Quickswood was extremely abstemious, like all his generation of the Cecil family.

and a High Churchman, he had no doubts of his authority in such matters. So by way of introducing the passage from the Gospel (Matthew 29:36) – 'I was naked and ye clothed me, hungry and ye fed me' – he announced, 'It reminds me of the passage through the House of Commons of the Aliens Act of 1911.' Or after Harvey's reading of Revelation 7:9 – 'I saw a great multitude which no man could *possibly* number' – 'Harvey, you are guilty of a *gross* liturgical error.' Walter, who tended to dislike the ritual of the Church, but had a deep interest in theology, found the morning excursus a good starting-point for the lunch-time debate. As time went on, the stimulus and enjoyment of his conversation came far to outweigh the irritations. Years later, Quickswood was to return to attend the funeral of his successor, Sir Henry Marten – formerly Vice-Provost and a man of extremely traditional outlook. When Walter was helping him down the steps of Chapel, Quickswood remarked apropos the traditional lesson – 'And I saw a new heaven and a new earth' – 'How Henry would hate that!'

John Wilkes, Walter's predecessor as Master-in-College for seven years, had been considered by the 'aesthetes' as an improvement, if a limited one, on H.K., by the intellectuals duller but less narrow-minded, and by the athletes a poor bargain. No one disliked him, for he was a most kindly man; but perhaps because he was shy he kept himself at a distance from his scholars, and he was thought nothing like so approachable as he later came to be at Radley.

Walter quickly won over all the Senior Collegers. A letter sent that autumn by R. H. Dundas from Christ Church, who had asked two very recent ex-Collegers to dine at High Table, tells how he had listened to their unrestricted praise for him – 'the best thing that has ever happened to College'. Yet there were no dramatic changes; indeed there were scarcely any visible changes at all. A Master-in-College could only work through his Sixth Form and boys are generally conservative of their customs and privileges. Walter's views, though rather more liberal then the narrow conservatism of most of the senior masters, were fundamentally traditional; he approved of order and discipline, and was quite happy to accept most of the customary practices. What Collegers thought of as a much more liberal regime seems to have been only a more measured and thoughtful approach to disciplinary problems.

He was barely a dozen years older than his Sixth Form, but not unusually young for a Master-in-College appointment, and they felt they could go to him for advice as one might go to an older brother or young uncle. That advice was given after reflection without any of the Olympian certainty which comes so easily to housemasters – causing the recipient to act in exactly the opposite manner. Walter was willing to listen to opposing views, being careful not to steer discussion too obviously the way he thought best. By using methods not very different from those of Socrates he would often lead boys to produce for themselves the solution they wanted, with the result that they found in him a source of reliable counsel! But he urged the importance of tolerance, even if he sometimes failed to show it himself. 'Cultivate the Broad Flexible Outlook' (or 'BFO'), he used to say. They came to recognise that, as well as believing in it himself, there were for him universal principles which informed and gave strength to his personality. 'No, that wouldn't be right', or 'It won't do' – often humorously, sometimes seriously, occasionally in deadly earnest.

With the younger boys he was less at ease. They were shy, so was he, and when he went round at nights with little over an hour to visit the majority of his charges, little wonder the conversation went no further than 'You all right?' 'Yes, Sir.' 'Good night then.' But Walter was quickly able to convey the impression that he knew most if not all of them well. One writes, 'In my first year I was in awe of him, but when I became Captain of Chamber I soon realised the depth of his concern

and knowledge of us.' Later on they learnt to appreciate his difficulties and wanted to help: some would think up a suitable
subject for debate with him in the passage. He told several in
after years how grateful he had been for this assistance.

Often-recalled features of life in College were the 'Secular
Singing' evenings. These were Saturday sing-songs of pieces
taken either from the *Oxford Song Book* or from popular songs
outside the Oxford collection, several of them from Gilbert
and Sullivan and one or two in Greek translations (attributed
by some to Ronnie Knox) such as 'Tit-Willow' or
'Clementine'. Attendance was entirely voluntary; usually
about thirty boys came from all stages of College and gave
tongue to their hearts' desire in the Master-in-College's
study. The evenings were particularly popular with boys in
Chamber who came in their dressing-gowns and were allowed
to stay up late. Francis Cruso or some other musical expert
would be invited to play the piano. There were normally no
solos, though when after a few years Walter was established,
he could occasionally be prevailed upon, feigning some
pretended hesitation, to sing. He had a limited repertoire of
rather gloomy songs which he sang, out of tune, with dolorous
gusto. His theme was for the most part mortification or death:
for example, the sad end of 'Little Billee' ('. . . so let's eat
he'), or from 'My Grandfather's Clock':

> Ninety years without slumbering, tick tock, tick tock,
> His life's seconds numbering, tick tock, tick tock,
> It stopped
> Short,
> Never to go again
> When the Old Man died . . .

or from 'The Beautiful Golden Frame' which Walter liked to
think of as his *pièce de résistance*:

> If those lips could only speak,
> If those eyes could only see,
> If those beautiful golden tresses
> Were there in realitee!

47

Could I only take your hand
As I did when you took my name –
But it's only a beautiful picture
In a beautiful golden frame ...

But there was with Walter a darker side. An Oppidan pupil remembers vividly his first encounter with Walter in Pupil Room. 'How have you been taught to pronounce Latin?' 'The right way, Sir.' 'Don't patronise *me*!' Though he rarely lost his temper with a boy he saw to it that they were aware of his displeasure. 'I'm really very vexed' was not too bad – the culprit could hope the sun would shine again: 'I'm passionately angry' was more serious. 'I'm black with passion' was threatening, and to escape without penalty was a rare triumph.

A Captain of the School recalls an evening when, having organised College prayers, he went out to a society meeting. Returning later, he first met Tim Burrows who warned that Walter was 'black with fury'. 'If you go to him and don't try to defend yourself it may be all right,' he said. At the end of the first line of the hymn, disaster had struck: 'Father we praise Thee now the night is o'er.' There was an instant roar: 'Stop the hymn,' cried Walter, 'No hymn.' By the time the Captain of School saw him he had calmed down, his anger having become a little synthetic. It was a side of Walter that was not without its absurdities. Then Walter had his favourites, boys who could 'get away with it', but were usually virtuous. His *bêtes noires* were generally contrary or unresponsive ones, and to these he could seem, and perhaps was, unfair. A very few, naturally enough, found Walter difficult to live with during their sojourn at Eton, and one – an academic in later life – could never bring himself to meet him again.

College was a clever, competitive community, the boys often spiking each other's guns. Walter's special strength was that, though sometimes emotionally upset, for most of the

Walter and Jane, West Highlands, 1950.

Left: *March, 1951.* Right: *Cuzco, Peru, 1961. Walter was travelling on behalf of the British Council.*

Westminster, about 1956.

time he seemed quite relaxed. Yet some in College thought he should have taken a more positive line in running it. However, it was still very much the Eton ethos that the best way to prepare boys for responsibilities they would have later was to give them all possible responsibility in their time in school – masters should stay in the background. In College, Sixth Form issued almost all edicts, even, in wartime, instructions in air-raid precautions; Walter hardly ever addressed College on routine matters. And, of course, the Sixth Form administered punishment, though Walter was consulted beforehand if beating was involved. The cane was very much less in evidence in his time in College, and he probably disapproved of it, but it was the generally accepted method of punishment for many offences, and Walter did not usually challenge tradition openly. His remaining in the background made some think that he did not know enough of what was going on, and in particular that he should have stopped instances of bullying much earlier. No housemaster could ever say with confidence 'There is no bullying in my house', but those who were in College during the fifteen years before Walter was in charge had very much greater cause for complaint. His friendly if somewhat brooding manner, his dislike of extremes, and his sage advice 'rubbed off' to a considerable extent on his senior boys.

In moments of personal crisis, however, there was no doubt that Walter was in charge. When, as did occasionally happen in the hothouse atmosphere of College, a young scholar developed a religious mania, and was found kneeling for hours before a cross in his room, the much-perturbed Captain of the School asked Walter what should be done. 'Oh, don't worry', Walter replied, 'I'll get him out of that all right.' In a more alarming episode, a boy burst into Walter's bedroom early one morning, announcing that he was the Second Person of the Trinity. 'But not before breakfast,' said Walter, emerging from the bedclothes – and this matter-of-fact answer checked the boy, who allowed himself to be sedated and taken to hospital. And when in the war a nearby bomb brought down most of the ceiling in the study, where Walter was giving a pupil back his verses – and his markbook still shows the traces – each was amazed, as they picked themselves up out of the debris, at the other's sang-froid. Years later, at Tim Burrows' memorial service, Walter said 'I have never known anyone I would rather have been bombed with.'

The outbreak of war had found Walter, like most of the younger masters, anxious to 'do his bit'. As a teacher and housemaster he was in a reserved occupation, but that did not satisfy him, especially when some of his first Collegers appeared in the casualty lists. From the Sixth Form that had welcomed him into College barely half survived. Those who never came back included all the leading figures, among them his first Captain, Henry Head – a Balliol scholar before he was seventeen – and perhaps the finest all-round athlete, Kenneth Hope-Jones, Eton had ever seen. Later on were even more grievous losses – amongst them Patrick Shaw Stewart, of whom he was particularly fond, the eldest of three much-liked brothers, and Richard Neville, one of his earliest Colleger members of A1. It took much patient argument to convince Walter that his continuing presence at Eton was essential for the school's academic coherence and a task more useful than the Services would be likely to find for him.

'As for the blitz, we took the whole period in our stride,' records one scholar, 'with its nightly air-raid alarms, its fairly frequent excursions to the air-raid shelter and the almost continuous tarry smell of the smoke which was being generated to screen the factories in Slough. During air-raid alerts it would be Walter's duty to patrol the College buildings. Two bombs, on successive days, fell on the College, destroying the Precentor's house in Weston's Yard, and then the Head Master's schoolroom and much of Upper School. On the following morning Walter found the Provost poking around amongst the debris with his umbrella, when he uncovered the tail-fin of an unexploded bomb. 'This one won't go off,' he said to Walter; 'It's a dud.' But it was a time-bomb and blasted out all the Chapel glass some hours later. Next morning was Founder's Day and chapel was held in a building without windows, amid piles of broken glass and in freezing cold. Not a reference was made at any point in the service to the fearsome events of the past two nights, and Walter realised, he said, for the first time, that Hitler was not going to be able to defeat the British. Meanwhile, little did he know of the increasing regard in which especially the senior boys had come to hold him. In 1942, one wrote a poem with him in mind:

Through the night and rain I blundered
With a better man than I;
In lightning and in thunder,
And the earth was like the sky.

There was no time then for talking
We could neither hear nor see;
I was glad that I was walking
With a better man than me.

Although no great enthusiast for games, Walter was expected to watch whatever contest his charges were engaged in, and in course of time he became quite a keen spectator. One day, at a cricket match, under a leaden summer sky, somebody apologised for the cold fruit juice, and was assured with mock solemnity, 'Nothing can quench the fire within.' Later he acquired a dog called Sam who soon picked up his master's taciturn manner. This was an advantage, as it enabled him to accompany Walter to the schoolroom, where he sat silently through the proceedings, neither asleep nor listening, but lost in sombre thought. Furthermore he was an unexpected bonus, for dog-owners had a higher standing in the eyes of

the Dames – matrons of the Oppidan houses – who were
compelled by loyalty to watch games of which they knew
nothing, but who had previously found Walter uncom-
municative. Sam broke the ice. He had spent his early years
in the West Highlands, where he had taken to chasing sheep
and had become unmanageable. In Eton's more sedate
atmosphere he came into his own. However, he never forgot
his past and Walter delighted in asserting that, when bored
of an afternoon, Sam was liable to walk into Windsor,
returning – on his own – by bus.

Walter would have liked to be good at games. Sometimes
he claimed to have represented Cambridge at lacrosse. But it
was the Wall Game which most excited him. When playing
in the position of Wall, his adult strength could shove
effectively – with surprising ferocity – against his younger
opponents. And he must have played fives, for on one
occasion he represented the Masters against the School; it
was wartime, when many young masters were away, and the
sixth pair failed to win a game. But it has to be said that
Walter showed little interest in the Arts. College had its
musicians but no Master-in-College since Crace, who loved
not only music but was a great university actor, had done
much to encourage them. So Walter's lukewarm support
aroused little resentment. It was the Head Master after all,
who opposed them. When asked if the College Music Society
could go after 'lock-up' to practise the *Messiah* in Chapel, he
grudgingly assented; 'though, mark you, if it hadn't been the
Messiah I would have said No.' The secretary of the Society,
a Colleger, knew Walter would never have said No.

In the evenings Walter was generally busy with his upper
boy pupils. As English was not taught as a separate subject,
a tutor would prepare his pupils for School Certificate, and,
in any case, was expected to encourage their reading habits.
Walter's own favourite authors were Johnson and
Wodehouse, but he found the former not much appreciated

by them, though Boswell was, and Wodehouse he thought they could read for themselves; whereas Jane Austen and Trollope, for example, they might well miss. Unlike those teaching English today, he rarely stopped to explain or to analyse; by reading aloud he hoped to stimulate them to read for themselves. Very occasionally he would relent and read the best of Wodehouse, but it was done with such enjoyment on his part (he could never resist chuckling at jokes, least of all his own) that the actual words were sometimes lost. He also prepared nearly all his pupils for Confirmation. Of such preparation it was said that it satisfied both practically and intellectually, and was in no sense emotive. The same could be said of his sermons, in which he never stooped to entertain. The first was preached at Radley, which contained the memorable words, uttered with particularly gloomy relish: 'For we know that we must all die.' 'He had invited some of us to come over with him in AMO 23,' writes one Colleger, 'perhaps to give moral support. He wanted to try his hand at preaching, to start with away from Eton. I suspect he was thinking of the possibility of headmastering even then, and may have talked to John Wilkes about it.'

A Johnsonian melancholy was part of Walter. It was one of the crosses he had to bear. As a rule he carried it lightly, making a joke of it by means of a gloomy pose and thus ridding himself of it with the help of other people's laughter or amusement. 'I'm feeling low' or 'rather vexed' meant that he needed cheering up, that nothing serious was wrong – it was his Eeyore role. So, on his thirty-fifth birthday, for instance, it was now 'half-time' or 'downhill all the way'. Or, in what was to be his last year when he thought there was a good chance of College winning the Wall Game on St Andrew's Day (victories on either side were rare), but the College Captain decided during the game that a win was not possible so forced a draw, Walter sulked – there is no other word for it – all through the supposedly festive lunch which followed. Then his neighbour, father of the culprit, asked, 'Are you not preaching in Chapel tomorrow?' 'Yes.' 'Then had you not better put yourself in a more cheerful frame of mind?' 'Yes, I suppose I had. Have some custard...!' And the meal went on.

One revealing aspect of the senior Collegers' affection was that some did their best to help Walter at the black times. Many boys would exploit a housemaster's weaknesses for their own ends, but not these: it might not be easy to cheer him up, they might just sit quietly with him, but they were pleased to be able to repay some of the debt they felt they owed him. One, however, does recall the irony of the situation, in that Walter was after all there to help them. Notwithstanding that, it is doubtful whether without weaknesses he would have won such high esteem. And they were the shadow of the man whose company they found highly congenial, not least when he 'let his hair down' – a favourite phrase – giving vent to some ridiculous event or point of view, made larger than life by his masterly way of putting things. For the most part he was open and steady, and meanwhile streets ahead intellectually of any of them. Those who combined affection with respect knew him for the vulnerable person he truly was.

Walter seems to have spent little of his holidays with his mother and father in London, although he never ceased to visit them regularly. People living in Catford in the war were amongst those most at risk from the German bombers as they neared their targets in the City and the London docks. From the outbreak of war until they were bombed out, his parents resisted his hopes of their moving out. Civilian casualties in SE6 during the blitz were heavy and they experienced the nightly, sometimes daily, warnings, the sounds of approaching aircraft, the ack-ack gunfire, and the crumps of bombs and land-mines. Walter's father continued to go as best he could to work, often without knowing what he would find when he got there.

On the night of 16 April 1941 two bombs fell in the garden of 89 Inchmery Road. Their craters were 'big enough to take a bus in each', wrote Walter. The house was a ruin and the Hamiltons were very lucky to survive. Walter went immediately to fetch them. A school property was found and the Eton community, led by Grizel and others, gave them a warm welcome. Walter was relieved and happy to have his parents living near by, and he was proud of them. They became quite familiar figures, although his father was the quicker to adapt and more sociable than his mother, whose health was beginning to fail. She died on Christmas Day 1943. From soon after their arrival Walter Hamilton Snr. was employed in the bursary, working in the accounts department, and he stayed on at Eton until his death in 1948. He blossomed during these years, and photographs of him show a remarkable likeness in physique to Walter, and in manner too.

Ella McCarthy had moved with the Hamiltons from Inchmery Road. She nursed Walter's mother through her last illness and looked after his father until he too died. She then returned to Catford, but when in 1950 Walter became Headmaster of Westminster Ella went again to assist. She stayed until after his marriage. However, she travelled to Mull every year after that, and was there as cook during the summer holidays until 1959, the last year of her life. She was a wonderful servant and friend to the Hamilton family.

No portrait of Walter during his years at Eton can be true to him without more account of his earlier holidays. Sometimes he made short visits to Cornwall and the Craces, or to the Lake District where he walked long distances. Or there was wartime harvesting (which he hated) or felling trees in Bagley Wood to make pit-props, with Richard Martineau and invited Collegers. On one West Somerset farm he enlivened the work of his gang by putting 'Dr Foster went to Gloucester' into Greek verse. On his way to another he came upon a notice which read, 'All applications for work on this new Sanatorium building should be addressed to the Clerk of the Dalwhinnie Estate', and instantly hailed it as an elegiac couplet. The same pupil who had found Walter so terrifying at their first encounter, now a senior and distinguished scholar, invited Walter to stay with his family in Co. Durham to help with the harvest. Having done so, he was filled with apprehension, for his father was very much a traditional hunting squire: in youth he had greatly disliked his housemaster ('The Ram' – A. B. Ramsay, later Master of Magdalene and considered by some the epitome of the scholar gentleman), and he had also found Cyril Alington, teaching him in Army Class, a 'sarcastic beggar'. What would he now make of Walter? He needn't have worried. Both recognized in the other the qualities of a proper man, and they became good friends.

But it was to Morar Lodge, near Arisaig on the north-west coast of Scotland, that Walter went for as much of the Easter and summer holidays as possible. This was the home of the Shaw Stewarts. All three boys were members of College, and their mother, Matty, made a habit of inviting her sons' schoolmasters to stay. Here he came to feel totally at home. Indeed his affection for the family and the place grew over many visits and was to last for the rest of his life. Later, Matty rented Walter the nearby Gatehouse of Traigh, and his manservant, Churchill, in College went there with his wife to keep house for him. Here Walter felt he had a home of his own, and it looked straight out to sea and the islands of Rhum and Eigg.

Gavin Maxwell describes Morar Lodge as it was in the mid-1940s:

'Probably' [he wrote in *Harpoon at a Venture*], it is impossible to describe Morar Lodge to anyone who did not know it ... In fiction perhaps, old Mrs Knox's house, as described in *The Experiences of an Irish RM*, approached it most nearly: its atmosphere of comfort, kindness, mingled with squalor and riches, but, above all, its animals ... The living-rooms were occupied by a numerous, indeterminate, and largely floating population of animals and dogs ... and the noise of their disagreements, attempted amours, and harsh protests was ... one of the more characteristic sounds of the house. [Of these dogs, Walter's Sam was one.]

Whereas there was definitely traceable farming activity at Morar Lodge, the pursuit of which occupied much of the family's waking hours, it was for their charm or pathos that the livestock was mainly selected ... Only one obvious animal was missing from that house, but there was evidence of its existence in the past, for on the shelf in the bathroom there stood for a long time a bottle labelled in faded ink 'Lotion for the donkey's eyes – I think'.

It was when Walter was staying at Morar Lodge that he first met Gavin. He was an immensely colourful character to whom Walter took an immediate liking. He had enormous charm, piercing blue eyes, and endless powers of not only believing in his own projects but of persuading others to believe in them too. He persuaded Walter, and a number of others, to invest £500 (most of his savings) to help him build a shark factory on the island of Soay. Gavin was convinced that a fortune could be made from any number of shark products. In the end, and long after Walter's association had finished, the project failed – principally because it had been overambitious.

Walter always said he would have liked to have been an Arctic explorer. Though never given the opportunity, he was drawn by a sense of adventure to the shark-fishing. Each foray lasted about a week. He used to describe how he and Gavin caught the sharks. So stupid were they, he claimed, that all they needed to do was to creep up behind them and

shove a harpoon in their side. This was an understatement.
The sharks, one moment their dorsal fins clearly visible,
would submerge without a ripple, they could change
direction unexpectedly, and poor visibility deceived the true
depth of a target more than twenty-five feet long and at least
five feet wide. 'The harpoon', writes Gavin, 'could have ten
feet of water to penetrate before reaching it' and 'when a
basking shark panics it can streak past on an opposite course,
almost too fast for the eye to follow.' Seas were gale-swept,
crew members were washed overboard and guns often
misfired. Such high adventure was quite aside from the
normal course of life: Walter could not have been happier.
He loved the excitement and he enjoyed too the fact that no
one would have expected the apparently conventional man
others believed him to be, to spend so much time on Gavin
Maxwell's *Sea Leopard*. And nobody was more amused or
proud of the story of him and Squeak, a local Highland
skipper, as told by Gavin:

> On this occasion when he came to Scalpay pier, Squeak leaned
> down from his bridge to see my guest, Walter Hamilton, whose
> head and shoulders were protruding from the after hatch of the
> *Sea Leopard*. Walter, usually a dignified and staid figure, wore a
> week's growth of beard, and was dressed in a black and white
> Faeroese sweater. His beard merged with his hair, which was
> standing on end, and he presented an entirely unscholastic
> appearance. When Squeak had first made his acquaintance on
> the mainland he had been engaged upon a translation of Plato's
> *Symposium*, a fact that had made a deep impression upon
> Squeak's unclassical mind.
>
> His eyes came out on stalks now, as he peered down, crimson
> and incredulous, and recognised Walter.
>
> 'Whatt are your doing hee-ar?' he shrilled. 'You look chust
> like a py-rate.' Then following no apparent train of thought:
> 'You'll be writing another book, I suppose.'

After each holiday the adventurer returned south,
reluctantly but refreshed, still the Highlander at heart. Few

who knew him both in term time and in the holidays were less than astonished at the contrast. It was never long before he yearned again for the hills and the sea.

Meanwhile his Eton 'charges' were scattered all over the world. The depth of their affection can be estimated from the many letters they wrote to him either during the holidays or after they left Eton. Most boys write at least once to a housemaster, rather stiff letters of thanks or asking if they can come for lunch. But these were utterly different, entirely natural letters as if written to a friend, telling how the goats, pigs and chickens were getting on – a wartime attempt to raise 'food on the hoof' – or describing life in wartime university while awaiting call-up. Once in the Services, especially while training, there was plenty of time to write, and letters to Walter were a good way of expressing their feelings. The other men on the assembly-line, the girls ('immoral harpies and not a bit attractive'), the sense of achieving something – all these are related in cheerful, or occasionally depressed, detail. Other letters came from what was obviously Italy or France or Palestine. There is a sheaf from the extreme north of Russia, where an old Colleger found himself as a rating in a sort of Naval Liaison Group. Almost every writer sent his love. Walter must have found time to reply to most of these with news of Eton or old friends.

When the war came to an end Walter is remembered dancing Sir Roger de Coverley in School Yard and, when at last College had gone to bed, opening a bottle of green Chartreuse, long stored, which he shared with his Sixth Form. In the general election which followed he told College that since he had three votes, two from Cambridge and one at Eton, he had been able to cast one for the Conservatives, one for the Liberals and one for Labour.

But by this time Walter must have decided that he needed a

change, if not something of a rest. He had been Master-in-College for eight years, and that was longer than most: he had turned down an invitation to stand for the headmastership of Harrow – because he couldn't leave College in wartime. He also rejected what was probably the opportunity of becoming Principal of Makerere, the University College in East Africa, on the rather prosaic grounds that, as he put it, he was 'not sure whether he would like African boys as much as English ones'; he certainly knew he would miss his friends – there was little of the educational idealist in Walter! Nor, with the end of the war, was he attracted by the idea of taking on an Oppidan house after College. Indeed there were some who thought he might not make a very good housemaster because he continued to find it hard to communicate with small boys; they believed he would make a better headmaster. In any event Eton did not exert so great a pull as it did for Richard Martineau and Francis Cruso, who never considered going elsewhere until their working lives were over; and if not apparently ambitious to others Walter was certainly sure that there was more important work he could do.

For the time being however he was weary from over five years of the war. Responsibility for the boys' safety (Collegers had slept underground for weeks at a time), fire-watching at night, extra teaching (beginners' German in his case) owing to fewer staff, war work in the holidays – these were on top of what had come to seem a relentless routine. Add to this the casualty lists, the recurring strain of saying good-bye to boys aged eighteen – wondering if he would ever see them again, writing to bereaved parents, and then his own bereavements. The best way to resolve his future, to give himself time to think and to take up again his work on Plato laid aside all these years, was to return to Trinity for a spell. Such a change would be better than a rest. So he told Claude Elliott that he wanted to leave Eton at the end of summer 1946 and would not be coming back.

The Collegers when they eventually heard the news were

horrified, but he explained to them that he would, in any case, have given up College very soon. His colleagues, and many retired masters too, expressed their regrets in terms much more moving than the conventional; one said that to be with Walter was his main reason for coming back to Eton from the Army. Jan Crace had moved from Cornwall to Henley, he wrote, not least to be nearer to Walter, and now he was moving farther away! Most appreciated why he was taking this step, unusual though it seemed: only Quickswood from his Bournemouth retreat wrote (or rather dictated, since his shaking hand was now unable to hold even a pencil) his full approval: he had always, he said, preferred undergraduates to boys. This letter is an indication of the regard the former Provost had for Walter; he had found little to talk about with Henry Marten, his Vice-Provost, who was very set in his ways, or with Elliott who was deaf and hated argument, or the Bursar, who never spoke (his wife made up for it), or the Lower Master, who was forcefully incoherent: Walter was the most congenial companion he had found at Eton.

That last Summer Half with its farewell dinners, its valedictory speeches and letters of regret from parents and old Collegers followed a predictable course. One of those most deeply affected, though that is not easy to discern in her long letter written at the beginning of the next Half, was 'the Airedale'. She had fed and managed College wonderfully during the war, with a ferocious devotion to duty, and spared Walter all those domestic worries that beset Oppidan housemasters; and clearly she had become very attached to Walter, who, in turn, had come to appreciate and admire her virtues.

No one wanted to see him go; in the relatively short time he had been at Eton he had shown himself not only the scholar he was known to be, but a man with an unusual capacity for friendship, with young and old, of great soundness of judgement and counsel, and with a cool head in a crisis. One devoted parent from the Eton years wrote, after Walter's death: 'I know he was a great scholar and administrator and distinguished himself in many ways, but I think perhaps his loving kindness to a frightened little boy and many other pupils was as important and lasting as anything in his devoted life.'

That he was an outstanding Master-in-College is the verdict not only of those who were boys at the time (they had no comparisons) but of contemporaries and successors. And although it is to anticipate, an unusual number of his group of Collegers went on to become distinguished adults (and that after fairly heavy war casualties), for apart from the usual quota of headmasters, professors and churchmen, there have been several judges, top civil servants (including a Cabinet Secretary and an ambassador), notable politicians, among them two ministers of the Crown, a Lord Mayor of London and a General. It is hard to escape the conclusion that much of his influence has lasted a lifetime. Nearly thirty years later, Walter was invited to become a Fellow of Eton, an honour almost never accorded to one who was not an Etonian. Several of his former pupils were to be Fellows with him, and no invitation gave him greater pleasure.

For Walter's part, Eton had provided him with his first real home. As he looked back he realised he had come to love the place. It had taken him into a wider fuller world, so that he now knew he could deal with people and make friends with them. He had come to like the easy style, even in the midst of wartime, and to realise he admired that intelligence and quickness, that civilised and special charm, wherever he found it.

In return he had taught with distinction, and had transformed College from the rather conventional and restricted 'Schcol House' it had become before 1937. For the boys who were in its senior echelons it had become not unlike a university College. And the Colleger who has said that Walter Hamilton was the first schoolmaster he had ever thought of as a friend is not alone.

4

FROM LETTERS BETWEEN FRIENDS

A War-time Correspondence

W. H. and James Duff

JAMES FITZJAMES DUFF WAS the second son of James Duff Duff, classical scholar and Fellow of Trinity. He was educated at Winchester and, after serving in the Royal Flying Corps in the First World War, he went up to Trinity on the classical scholarship he had won at the age of sixteen. Ten years older than Walter, their friendship spanned forty years.

A warm admirer of the grammar school, James became a very successful lecturer and tutor to those seeking teaching careers in those schools, alternating between Armstrong College, Newcastle upon Tyne, and the University of Manchester.

In 1937 he became Warden of the Durham Colleges, then small in scale but which, after 1945, he developed so that later they had a full range of departments so that, when divided from the Colleges in Newcastle, they could stand as a university on their own. In 1949 he was knighted. His experience in education and university government made him widely sought after. He travelled abroad on public service in the Commonwealth, and he excelled as a public speaker.

His entry in the *DNB*, contributed by Walter, includes the following extracts:

The imposition of a new Warden from above was not wholly welcome, and it needed wisdom, vision, and much tact to set the

Colleges on the course of expansion necessary for their survival. He possessed these qualities abundantly, and with them a style of humour which could often win an argument or help to solve a problem by a sense of the ludicrous.

He combined a keen, lucid, and well-stored mind with a commanding personality. Always completely master of the business in hand and intolerant of anything bogus or pretentious, he was a formidable chairman and could be a ruthless interviewer; even on informal occasions his ripostes could be devastating. But they left no sting, and the warmth of his personal interest and the breadth of his sympathy won him great affection, especially from the young.

James Duff was physically unhandy – he never drove a car and in later life was a notably incompetent golfer – he made his mark by his style of conversation, an inimitable mixture of quotation, banter, and sheer nonsense, with which he delighted his friends to the end of his life.

He died in 1970 at the age of seventy-two. He was unmarried.

The letters which follow are from a correspondence which lasted intermittently for nearly forty years. Walter writes from Eton and James Duff from Durham.

1. *The Coming of War*

2nd October 1938

My dear James,

I have long intended to answer your letter, but really have not had the heart, let alone the time, to do so for the last fortnight. Now that it appears that our holiday was perhaps not after all quite our last, and that there is still hope of the Orkneys, I must say that it was one of the best holidays and that I enjoyed the chauffeurage as much as anything.

After leaving I had a quiet fortnight in Norfolk, and then quite a lot of work, as far as one could be quiet with the news getting daily worse. At the beginning of last week I definitely abandoned hope, and applied myself with energy to the construction of sandbag walls. Now, I think of having them pulled down to the sound of the flute, like the Athenians in 404.

I hope that you agree with me in being hopeful about this settlement.[2] It seems to me that public opinion in Germany probably stopped this war as much as anything, and that this is the first time that such a thing has ever happened. Why shouldn't it happen again? It is an enormous advance on 1914 and I can't think that it has really set up a dictatorial stock. One does not turn an ultimatum into a penultimatum without some loss of dignity. And can you conceive anything more fantastic than the Germans wildly cheering the Prime Minister of a country with which they might easily have been at war in a couple of days?

Politics are not really my thing, nor are sandbag walls. So I shall now go back, as a much greater man said, 'With relief and thankfulness,' to my proper job.

Yours,
Walter.

4th October 1938

My dear Walter,

Many thanks for your letter. There seems an extraordinary gulf between this time and three weeks ago. It feels like years; and I feel old! I have never been in such misery as I was last week, and the necessity (which you must have shared) of keeping some sort of face, to hearten one's 'flock', was sheer agony. I put all the office staff on to trench-digging and joined them when I could – much the most soothing occupation of those days. Not that Durham is a likely target, but it was something to *do*. It wasn't war itself, foul as it is,

---

[2]Munich.

but the hopeless evil results after a war, even a short and successful war, that formed the worst part of my own nightmare.

Well, the relief is enormous, but even apart from my relief, I entirely agree with you in being hopeful about the future. Dictatorship has had a blow, and public opinion showed it would not stand a general war, both in Germany and Italy. Enormously hopeful, that is. After all their filthy propaganda too. Chamberlain is a great man, and if he thinks our best chance of humanising Germany is to strike Hitler instead of soothing him, I am perfectly ready to trust him. We fought four years to make the Germans be different, and the only result was Nazism. That is what makes me think Chamberlain is probably right, though the difficulties are great.

Oh for next August.

Love,
James.

18th June 1939

My dear James,

My mother and father both think of going for a holiday at the beginning of August, the latter for the first time for years, and that means that I shall be wanted to drive them about until August 19th. But immediately after that I shall be as free as air, and I should like to have three weeks, or as long as you can manage. However, the Orkneys are not the place for a long stay for people like us, but, if we have three weeks, as I hope we shall, we might make a short dash for them. I should like to see the cliffs of Hoy and Kirkwall Cathedral. Still, that doesn't matter. The important thing is that I should have as long a holiday as possible with you. It is impossible not to be terribly disillusioned about Munich, though I still think that it was the right thing to do. But I still have feelings that if Adolf really meant to have a war, he would not wait while the forces against him proved stronger and stronger. But God knows how it will end. I hide my feelings pretty well and bear up, on the whole, surprisingly.

Thinking of Scotland is almost intolerable on an Eton Sunday afternoon, the nadir of the week.

Yours,
Walter.

28th August 1939

My dear Walter,

What strange times! I continue without the slightest hope of peace (though with considerable hope of what may happen in Germany very soon after war starts).

Last night I met Dr Goebbels, who let it out that Germany would invade Denmark today; he begged me not to give this away and left me; I rushed to telephone Lord Halifax, but my frantic appeals to the operator failed to get me through – and I woke up in a state of great distress. Did you think, on starting to read this paragraph, that the crisis has been too much for my reason? I hope you are not off your sleep. I am not, and that has been my only nightmare so far. I think often of Loch Duich, of Eigg, of Rhum, as we saw them on our way up from Glenelg – of the Totaig boat that evening, with the Five Sisters on one hand and sunset of the Cuillins on the other. A most memorable day, quite apart from the likelihood that it was the last reasonably care-free day of an epoch.

Here's to the day when we next cross Carter Bar northwards 'in the body or without it'. I hope for the former; but if not, please arrange for your spirit to meet mine at Totaig, a better place than the Moon, where I think you told me Plutarch located the disembodied.

Love,
James.

1st September 1939

My dear Walter,

So it's come, and, odd or even immoral as it may be, I am happier than I have been for months. I knew in my bones that it was coming, so this ends a long suspense. And it starts in circumstances of such infamy for the German government – exceptionally so even for them – that it is inconceivable that their nation is wholehearted. Ours is, as far as I can see, astonishingly so.

Many things remain to be seen in the next few days: Russia? Mussolini? Germany itself? USA? But it means the end of Hitler, even if it is a bloodier process than I am inclined to think. And that's worth any agony to achieve.

Love,
James,

2. The Phoney War

3rd September 1939

My dear James,

Well, here we are and what a relief! Like you I have never had the slightest real hope of peace since I left you, but I think there is some chance of a shortish war, and I am now almost cheerful, but for my parents being in London. Today is Cromwell's 'crowning mercy' day, Dunbar and Worcester. What omen do you draw from that?

I have not lost my sleep, chiefly because I have been incessantly occupied all day, building sandbag walls and helping to receive refugees at the station, carrying babies etc. I haven't actually got them in College, and we hope to open as usual, but we shall know better what we can do after a few air-raids.

Coleridge and Cruso are staying with me, which is a great comfort. Being alone is now the only thing I dread, that and the possibility of my running away if I get into the army. By the way, I observe that being over thirty-one I am too old for a commission without special qualification, which I can hardly be said to possess. But I am not worrying much about that. I shall do what I am told.

My wobbly writing is due to my having sat on a ladder all morning hurling up sandbags.

I believe that the war may drive me into Orders if I survive it, and thus your prophecy would be signally fulfilled. I really do feel that we are fighting against the power of evil and that nothing but Christianity, as you say, of a simple kind, can see us through. I am much encouraged by the entire absence of false heroics with which we are embarking on it.

Write again, and so will I.

Much love from
Walter.

24th September 1939

My dear James,

I have had the boys back since Wednesday, and feel much better. Before that I spent a period attempting to darken the whole of College which aroused me to a pitch of irritation I have never known before, but I am now quite cheerful. Francis Cruso is living with me to help in air-raids. We had to have the boys up last night on a bogus alarm by way of practice; it cheered me that they carried out their instructions with complete calm and efficiency, and dressed and reached their shelter in four minutes.

I still believe that this is going to be a long war, and if the Russians move it is probably a blessing in disguise. I cannot think that the German army will have enjoyed capturing Polish provinces, only to see them handed over to Russia. My present feeling is that there will soon be an abortive attack by Germany in the west, but Germany will then have an absolutely bloody winter and that there will be revolution in the spring. Is this wishful thinking? As for air-raids, if they don't start soon, I shall think that it is because they are terrified of reprisals.

I observe with interest that I am embarking on my confirmation class with more conviction than ever before. Does this seem to you to indicate that the beating of the wings of dog-collars can almost be heard?

David Graham-Campbell, having joined some reserve in the summer without telling anyone, is off on October 1st to train. Emotionally I feel that I ought to be doing the same, but they wouldn't look at me at present, and rationally speaking, I am afraid they are right. But if the war lasts for years I cannot stay here.

Love,
Walter.

3rd December 1939

My dear James,

The most depressing thing (for everything else has been astonishingly normal) has been the constant visits of chaps in uniform, some of them pretty gloomy, especially the embryo pilots. I had one of the latter staying with me last weekend who felt sure that he was going to be killed, and it was very difficult to administer consolation.

The boys are admirable. Like your young men they seem to have no illusions either about the necessity or the foulness of the war. And I, like you, am thoroughly wholehearted. If this isn't the power of evil I should like to know what is. The Russian invasion of Finland makes me feel positively sick, but at any rate it must be very upsetting to the Germans – the silence of the German newspapers seems to prove that. I shouldn't be really surprised at a coup by the Army and I am told today on good authority that we can already cope with the magnetic mine, and have found a way of exploding them from a mile off. So I do not think Adolf can be at all happy, and I don't believe he knows what to do next.

Write again.

Love,
Walter.

5th January 1940

My dear James,

I am not alarmed by your religious tendencies. I notice much the same thing in myself, and perhaps the dog-collar you foretold is drawing nearer. But I shall not assume it is so long as I am in College because I am sure that it would create an artificial barrier between me and the boys. However, I feel like you that it is Christianity or nothing in the world now.

I have been at home for a fortnight, except for a brief trip to Kent, and find my parents, especially my mother, rather oppressed by the war, and in need of cheering, which is why I have not gone away before, though I go tomorrow. Personally, I am not very unhappy about the war, though the Russians make my blood boil even more than the Germans. Why are earthquakes almost always in the wrong places?

I think the scuttling of the *Graf Spee* ought to have a good effect. The *Achilles* is commanded by one of my nicest parents, and I look forward to hearing about it; and the Germans cannot be very happy at the demonstration of Russian incompetence in Finland. What excellent people the Finns are.

I think of Loch Duich a good deal and particularly, for some reason, of the view across to Skye at Kyle Rhea. I will make a vow to go there every year in future if this war turns out all right. Let me hear from you.

Love,
Walter.

25th January 1940

My dear Walter,

Have I told you my sufferings on the Conscientious Objector's Tribunal? It is a loathsome job, and the presiding Judge doesn't improve things by constantly losing his temper. It has, very rarely, a bright moment; as today, when one eccentric youth came before us, and the more we asked him about warfare, the more loudly he talked about *birth-control*. 'As long as you sell contraceptives,' he cried, 'I shall resist all efforts to coerce me.' Even the grim cranks who filled the courts were dissolved in laughter. 1 per cent of those we see are the salt of the earth; 30 per cent are the scum of the earth. In between are a large number of chapel-headed fundamentalists and futile sentimentalists.

Dog-collar? 'I can almost hear the beating of its wings,' as John Bright said. Like you, I could not do my job here decently in a dog-hat and collar. But I do not think it inconceivable that I should chuck up this job, after the war or in the course of an interminable war, and close the university down, and seek a parish of Durham miners. But I am further from it than you. I am so very casual!

Love,
James.

17th March 1940

My dear James,

I have had what I can only call a gloomy Half, chiefly because one of my boys became very ill about a month ago, and a fortnight later died of pneumonia. I think I managed to keep my equilibrium fairly well in public, but combined with everything else it threw me into the worst gloom I have had since the war began. However, I am now better, though not exactly happy.

The idea of Hitler and Mussolini meeting at the top of the

Brenner is much more ridiculous than alarming somehow.

Did I tell you that I am now senior Divinity master? Another of my little wartime jobs is to teach beginners' German for four hours a week.

How good it would be to see Loch Duich, now alas a prohibited area.

Love,
Walter.

3. *The Battle of Britain*

20th June 1940

My dear James,

Well, a good deal of water has flowed under the bridge since I wrote to you last. What a frightful series of mostly avoidable disasters! However, for no very rational reason, I feel much better now, and full of hope that we shall fix them in the end. Some things, e.g. the last years of the Roman Republic, I have found it impossible to teach and the boys to learn, but I have managed to fall back on a lot of poetry, ancient and modern, and on the whole we are keeping our end up pretty well and propose to remain where we are unless we are told not to. I have lost three boys from panic, but otherwise my flock is intact. We haven't had an air-raid warning yet, you no doubt have had several. I anticipate a series of large attacks on London, but I think that we shall deal with them.

What will happen when the Half comes to an end I have no idea. I shall either go and farm with some of the Sixth Form boys, or become a Local Defence Volunteer and stay here. Lots of boys are doing the latter, and I have refreshed my knowledge of the mechanism of the rifle, which doesn't seem to have changed in the last fourteen years. I shall be registering next month but I do not suppose that I shall be allowed to become a soldier.

Love from Walter.

23 June 1940

My dear Walter,

Your letter was extremely welcome. I started writing to you about a week ago, but my gloom was such that I could not get on with it. I asked my oldest and wisest colleague the other day, in strict confidence, whether he still thought we could win the war, and he said, 'No, I don't really, but I'm going to go on saying we shall.' And, in equally strict confidence to you, I feel much the same. I think that we can go on resisting for a long time, perhaps indefinitely; and miracles may always happen. But that is as far as I can go. I want to be killed rather than survive the loss of the war – and that although I know in my bones that a thing so negative and self-consuming as Nazism *cannot* win a lasting victory. But I have not the courage even to face the temporary victory thereof and its consequences.

Moods? Black misery intermittently but not all the time. A good deal of rabid fury – today it has taken the form of Italy dictating terms to France. A certain amount of elation at our plight; I don't know why, unless it is what martyrs felt at the stake! I have taken to prayer, but not to fasting.

Much love,
James.

11th August 1940

My dear Walter,

My *morale* has improved since France collapsed! I don't know why, unless it is that instead of the great wave of defeatism which I expected then, people of all sorts are clearly much more resolute than they were – and that is not simply because the invasion hangs fire or because our RAF is doing so well; it was noticeably too early for either of these to account for it. I still don't see how to win the war! But it would almost be true to say that I don't care. Fighting Hitler (and Musso) is a good enough programme. *And* Japan, *and*

Russia, if need be. I am prouder of being British than I ever was before.

Love,
James.

14th August 1940

My dear James,

I write this, curiously enough, at 4 a.m. sitting in a sort of porter's lodge in charge of the Radley siren. I came here last Saturday with Richard Martineau and eight of my boys, to engage in forestry in a place called Bagley Wood. The work is not unpleasant, and very well-run, and anyhow it is a change, and if one is going to be a lumber-jack conditions could not be better.

Apart from this I have been at Eton for a fortnight, being a fireman, so that the regular members of the AFS may have some sort of holiday. The result of the first fortnight's intensive practice is that I have become Captain of the corresponding thing here for the duration of my stay!

Isn't it very odd how quickly one becomes accustomed to things? The possibility of invasion worries me surprisingly little. And there is, as you say, a certain feeling of comfort in the fact that we are now depending on ourselves and in the same boat, soldiers and civilians alike. I have an unreasonable conviction that we shall win, and it is growing stronger. The only thing that I feel quite intolerable is the contemplation of the behaviour of the Government all last winter, and the behaviour of the French now. I do not think that there has ever been such an act of treachery by a whole nation.

Much love,
Walter.

2nd September 1940

My dear James,

I wish that I could come to Durham. But now I am back at Eton to do another fortnight as an auxiliary fireman, I do not feel that I can go as far from home as Durham. Since I came here last Friday there have been about a dozen air-raids and a good many bombs promiscuously dropped, and some within a mile or so of us. My mother bears up very well, but I do not think that she would like to have me too far away.

The prospect of being killed worries me very little, although I passionately want to see what is going to happen, and I think that one is probably in a better position for seeing that in this world than in the next. And I don't care what happens if only we can get the brutes down, and I believe that we shall. I should like to show the French too, what we can do without them. I am inclined to think I dislike them almost more than the Germans.

Love,
Walter.

2nd October 1940

My dear Walter,

I expect you have had sorrows by now, from casualties among recent boys. I was lucky in that way till a fortnight ago when I had a blow which I mind more than I thought I should. My clerk, a lad I appointed soon after I came here – character pure gold – I liked him very much from the first; I should have said that he had all virtues (and great charm) except the military one; I thought him too gentle and too scholarly to be warlike. He had left school at 14, yet he read more and thought more than most of my undergraduates. Then war came, and on the first day of the war he joined the Air Force. His letters during his training course were a delight, especially the last when he had joined an 'operational' squadron and began active service in a bomber. After just a month of active service he was killed on his way back from a bombing-raid. I wonder if you saw him ever, a fresh faced, yellow-haired youngster with a rather shy manner. They brought him back here for burial, and at the funeral I wished passionately that I could change places with him, and be safely and most honourably dead, leaving him a life ahead of him. Sergeant Stanley Bews – honour his name for a moment, since so few people will.

I wonder if you have evacuated your parents from London?

Love,
James.

4. *'The Blitz'*

8th January 1941

My dear James,

You know what the end of my Half is like and this time it was aggravated by bombs. The subsequent period was spent by College dotted in twos and threes among the Oppidan houses, and by me with the Head Master, who had most of my small boys sleeping on his dining-room floor. Most of my ceilings were down, but I got back into my house in time to have my parents to stay with me for a week at Christmas, and College itself will be all right for next Half if Goering doesn't do it again. Considering that almost all the boys' ceilings came down, and all the windows in Weston's Yard were blown in, it was really remarkable that no one was even hurt. The damage to Upper School should not be ultimately irreparable, but the Savile House bomb destroyed what was, I think, the most beautiful room in Eton.

The bomb has shaken me a little, not in regard to my own safety, but to that of my charges, especially the small ones. If any of them were killed, I should feel as you felt about your clerk; what you said about him moved me much . . .

My parents obstinately refuse to leave their house in London, and that too is a trouble. They are perfectly cheerful and take the view of Socrates that when one is seventy it doesn't much matter what happens. And I think there is a good deal to be said for that.

I have just heard of an old countryman whose reaction to the siren is to put his head under the bedclothes and to murmur 'Safe in the arms of Jesus and to 'ell with 'itler'. I think I shall do the same.

Much love,
Walter.

19th April 1941

My dear James,

My parents' house in London was bombed on Wednesday night. I am glad to say that they weren't hurt, and they are now here with me; but the house is an indescribable mess, with two craters in its small garden, into each of which I should think that you could put a bus. The immediate problem is to find them somewhere to live, which isn't easy.

However these things happen, and I am glad to have got them out of London, however forcibly.

Much love,
Walter.

22nd April 1941

My dear Walter,

What rotten luck. I am so sorry, while thankful that none of you were hurt ... I hope you will find a home for your parents without too much difficulty. I could put up one but not both, which I am afraid is a futile idea. But if it's any good, do say so.

If I had been twice bombed, like you, I think I should retire to Seatoller or the United States for six months or so. 'These things happen', you say; but they don't happen here in Durham, and I am becoming half ashamed of our security.

Much love,
James.

5. *Widening Horizons and Bereavement*

5th January 1942

Dear James,

I haven't been very gay, but I am pretty confident about the course of the war. Last Half was foul, nothing but row after row, and in Christmas week I heard of the death of two pupils, one (aged nineteen) in the *Prince of Wales* and another in Libya. Since then I have had staying with me on his last leave before going to sea the son[3] of the Governor of Hong Kong, one of the nicest boys I have ever had, and I am oppressed with the horrible feeling that I shall probably never see him again. But one mustn't encourage such thoughts, and I do now think that the end is more or less in sight in spite of the Japanese. They remind me more than anything else of the Martians in the *War of the Worlds*.

Did I tell you that I have become a member of the Council and the Scholarship committee of the Kitchener Memorial Fund? The chairman of the latter is the Warden of Winchester. It should be quite interesting, especially after the war, but as most of the other councillors are peers and generals it is rather odd company for me.

I suppose I am a stick-on at Eton, but at the moment I have a passionate desire to get into something dangerous. I haven't heard a siren for about six months.

Much love,
Walter.

12th April 1942

Dear James,

This will be only a brief note as I am in the midst of reports. But I want your advice. Jim Butler has asked me to stand for the headship of Harrow. My first reaction is to refuse out of hand, but perhaps one ought to do adventurous and risky things, and I don't mean to stay at Eton forever.

[3]Brian Young

80

On the other hand, I am probably not the man to revivify a dying school. Please send me your thoughts on the subject.

Next week and the next I have Kitchener meetings in London, and shall be at Eton; then I am taking some boys to Cornwall for ten days.

Much love,
Walter.

14th April 1942

My dear Walter,

I've always disliked Harrow so much that my opinion is prejudiced. But I think you would find Harrow parents, Harrow staff, and Old Harrovians equally detestable; and what you as Headmaster could do for the boys under these conditions I hardly see.

That would be so even if Harrow were not moribund. It seems able to stand a vast deal of moribundity. Except for Montague Butler's headship, Harrow has been in bad odour for well over a century; yet it goes on, and not only goes on but continues to produce Prime Ministers and Masters of Trinity. Yet by what I hear – which isn't much and you undoubtedly know more – it's in horribly deep water just now. It seems to me they want not so much a Headmaster as an undertaker, or an emigration agent, to close the school down or take it out into the country and amalgamate it with Stowe – which might then add a flavour of Harrow-on-the-Hill to itself by taking the name of Stowe-on-the-Wold.

I *cannot* see a decent future for Harrow, where it is. It must add to the horror of the thing that they have to keep up the pretence, and expense, of being the second school in England, when in fact they are almost infamous.

So I should say 'no'. I agree that you shouldn't stay *very* much longer at Eton; there are twenty schools whose headship would be a more hopeful affair than Harrow's.

Love,
James.

28th December 1943

My dear James,

I know you will be very sorry to hear that my mother died on Christmas morning after quite a short illness. On December the 6th she began to ramble in her mind, but was quite happy and went on coming down as usual; then at the beginning of last week she became very ill, and after several days unconsciousness died very peacefully.

You will imagine that this leaves a great blank, but both my father and I are very glad that she did not linger in the state that she was in earlier in the month, and there is much to be thankful for. My good aunt is here, and has been a great comfort, and my father means to go on living here helping the bursar, and also his own admirable maid to keep house for him. So things might be worse.

I did not put in for Repton. I talked to the Headmaster about it, and he put no obstacles in my way, but told me that Shrewsbury will shortly be vacant and had been enquiring after me. I should prefer that, I think, and, as things are, I am glad not to have an immediate change in prospect.

My mother's funeral is tomorrow, in the side-chapel of College Chapel.

Much love, Walter

15th January 1945

My dear James,

About the chair.[4] I have thought of it a lot, but I don't really think it's for me. I feel in my bones that I had better stick to schoolmastering. Probably this is a sign that I am already unfitted myself for a change, but when I call vividly to mind the contrast between boys and the classes I had at Manchester, I don't think that I could bear to change, tempting as the prospect is in many ways.

---

[4] W.H. refers to the chair of classics at Durham

Do you know one John Morrison, a fellow of Trinity and now directing the affairs of the British Council in Jerusalem? He's about thirty-two, and an admirable chap in every way. No kinks of any kind. He might be the man for you, I think, and he wants to come home this coming year. Patrick knows all about him. Elliott is trying to get him here, but I think Durham might suit him better than a junior mastership, as he's married with two children. And he has more taste for research than I, but it's under control.

Much love, Walter.

3rd February 1945

My dear James,

This is a difficult question. I don't know anything about Morrison as a teacher, of course, but I should say that he would be good on the literary side. He certainly isn't a mere pedant in his special subject: indeed I should say that his merit is that he has a robust general interest in what one may call the humanities. If I were a headmaster, I would cheerfully give him my Sixth Form to teach, and one cannot say fairer than that. As for composition, he isn't absolutely first-class – I don't think he won a university scholarship – but he is good enough, and he would certainly get better by teaching. The only thing that I can say for myself is that I am a far better versifier than when I came to Eton.

Love, Walter.

6.   *What To Do Next*

10th April 1945

Dear James,

I am afraid that I shall not get in a visit to Durham this time. It is far too long since I have been, I know, but this is a tiresomely short holiday and I have to hang about to elect Kitchener Scholars next week. When that is done I mean to

83

make a dash to Morar with my dog, and sniff Highland air for ten days before the Half begins.

Yes, I have accepted Trinity (for October 1946, provisionally). I shall hate leaving College, and I fully agree with what you say about the lack of a flock, but I do feel that a breathing-space of two or three years would be a godsend, even if after that I go out into the world again. I certainly shan't refuse to do so if anything comes my way. But I am sure that I am right not to have an Oppidan house. I still think that I should like a headmastership, but I should like to come to it fresher than I am now, and I cannot bear the idea of touting about for one.

I am very glad you have got John Morrison. I am sure he will be good.

Much love, Walter.

31st October 1945

My dear James,

A letter came from a chap in the Colonial Office this morning asking me if I would stand for the job of Principal of Makerere.[5] I don't suppose you are behind this, you would have said so. But why should anyone else think of me?

I don't feel in my heart that this is my cup of tea, but on the other hand it is obviously a job worth doing, and I tend to believe that one ought to do what comes one's way. Obviously you are far better able to give advice on this subject than anyone else, so do send me your considered opinion on my suitability for the job. My present inclination is to say no, but I am quite ready to consider the matter seriously. It would certainly be a great and exciting adventure, and in that way it rather attracts me.

Love from Walter.

---

[5]Now the University College of East Africa

16th November 1945

My dear James,

Thank you very much for your extremely helpful letter. I have thought about the matter a lot, but I am afraid that I cannot bring myself to go. I don't suppose you will be surprised.

Whether I could take the same sort of interest in black boys as in Collegers I just don't know, and I imagine nobody could know until he tried. I don't see why I shouldn't, and it isn't that that stops me. But your remark about equability is very much to the point. I am not really very equable, and my gloom, so comic, is occasionally genuine, and if I could not dispel it by congenial company I might be wretched and therefore useless.

There is also the point that I don't like the danger of discovering, say in ten years time, on returning to England, that everyone has forgotten me. If I had a family it would be different, but I depend so much on my friends that this seems a serious objection. It would be bound to happen as far as my Eton connections were concerned, and I should hate to lose sight of all my young men. And I shouldn't be smiled on by Trinity, and I think that they would have some justification.

I can't help thinking that if I were a better man I should go, but, as things are, I don't feel sure enough of being successful or even of liking the job to take these risks.

Love from Walter.

1st February 1946

My dear James,

I expect that you have seen that the headmastership of Winchester has been advertised. I should like to try, but there is, of course, an awkwardness about Trinity. I don't really think it at all likely that I should get it – Christie, for example, is probably the sort of person they want – and the question is, is it worth upsetting them at Cambridge on what is probably a wild-goose chase? I should very much value your advice.

I wish you were a Fellow of Winchester. If I do apply, may I name you as one of my referees? If you think the whole idea preposterous, please say so.

Yours ever,
Walter.

6th March 1946

My dear James,

Of course, I took your excellent advice about Winchester. Very many thanks for it. I understand that I have also been named to them from another quarter, Jasper Ridley, one of the Fellows of Eton, but I haven't heard anything further about it, and I don't suppose that I shall.

Love from Walter.

28th March 1946

My dear James,

Very many thanks for your consolation. I don't really feel in the least cast down, because it never seemed more than the dimmest of possibilities. And I am quite looking forward to Trinity, partly because I am beginning to feel pretty well exhausted here. But I quite agree with you that I shall have failed if I stay at Trinity forever.

I hope that John Morrison is doing well.

Love, Walter.

18th July 1946

Dear Walter,

I enjoyed my visit as I always do when I come to stay with you. It is most melancholy to think that this is the end of your time as Master-in-College. You spoke of your future in terms of possible non-success at 'getting things'. But if I had your record of nine years doing a job quite incredibly well, I would lie back and leave instructions for that to be carved on my tombstone as a sufficient justification for my life. I would indeed.

Not that I really forecast a duller future for you. Far from it. I only envy you your power, for the rest of your life, to look back on your years in College with what ought to be unbounded pride and happiness.

Now go and do likewise at Trinity. You will, though I don't know how.

Love, James.

5

POST-WAR TRINITY

W.H.: Fellow and Classical Lecturer 1946–50; Tutor 1947–50;
University Lecturer in Classics 1947–50.

Memories of an Undergraduate

Tom Faber

Looking back after an interval of forty years it seems to me that Walter, who had no responsibility whatever for my welfare, was the first don I encountered as an undergraduate at Trinity to show any inclination to spend a moment longer in my company than was strictly necessary.

I first arrived as an insignificant scholarship candidate in March 1945, to spend an excessively uncomfortable week sharing a beautiful but ice-cold set in Neville's Court with a boy from another school. We saw nobody there but a tyrannical bedmaker, about four feet high and the same in diameter, who threatened to ruin my future career by reporting me for stealing, because on the first day I used a thin sliver of soap which the room's term-time inhabitants had left behind. Soap being rationed at the time, and having brought none with me, I remained unwashed for the rest of the week. Only at the end of it did we discover that the bedmaker was supposed to have supplied us with coal; no doubt she had found a better use for this in her own home.

Having been coached very systematically at school I passed Part I of the Natural Sciences Tripos in the summer of 1947 without difficulty, indeed with some distinction, but without having developed in any other way. I remained a tongue-tied schoolboy with rather few friends, in a university largely populated by students very much older than myself who had fought through the war and who, in their determination to work their way back into civilian life, had little time for youthful frivolity. My abiding memories of my first two years at Trinity are of struggling to keep warm in cold weather; of queuing on the stairs outside the kitchen office in the hope of obtaining one bottle of mediocre sherry to last one through a term; of queuing outside Fitzbillies in the hope of securing a lardy cake wherewith to supplement the dreary food dispensed in the College Hall, while long-standing residents of Cambridge walked past into the side entrance of the shop and emerged looking furtive, with their weekly orders concealed in bulging shopping-bags; of buildings, trees, gardens and a river whose beauty stirred me every day; and of glimpses from a distance of dons of legendary distinction.

G. M. Trevelyan, the Master, presided regularly in Hall – though not over the 6.30 and 7.15 sittings which undergraduates in their first and second years respectively were required to attend. Knowledgeable undergraduates could point to Wittgenstein in Trinity Street, as he disappeared into Matthews's tea shop. One mathematical giant, Professor Hardy, sat in a deckchair under the Trinity clock tower on sunny days, swathed in blankets; another, Professor Littlewood, walked two hundred yards across the Great Court in his dressing-gown every morning to visit the baths on I staircase, rather than use the bath installed for his benefit in Neville's Court. Professor Aston, whose work on isotopes was described in my physics textbooks, shared the services of his bedmaker with me and David Oates; she came in one morning in a fine fluster, having discovered Aston on the floor, and told us that she 'thought he was dead the way he was breathing'. Professor Dirac, though not a Fellow of Trinity, lectured on Quantum Mechanics to anyone who cared to attend – as I did in my third year for a while.

It was through David Oates, with whom I shared a set for two years, that I first met Walter. Walter was David's tutor, and because David was reading Classics he went to Walter for supervision as well. He was invited, at Walter's suggestion, to attend the Lake Hunt in June 1947, and the following year I attended the Lake Hunt too. There, during my time as a research student, I got to know Walter well, and a group of other dons besides.

The Lake Hunt was a Trinity institution, encrusted by sixty years of tradition sedulously fostered by its own Master, Patrick Duff, with the support at that time of several other Fellows, especially Outram Evennett, Kitson Clark, Walter, Mark Pryor, John Morrison and Andrew Huxley. Those lucky enough to be invited assembled outside the Great Gate at 6.30 a.m. on the Saturday morning after General Admission, to be driven up the Great North Road to Seatoller House in Borrowdale, sometimes by Walter but more often in the ancient Austins owned by Patrick and Outram. The journey was a slow one. There were no bypasses on the A1 in those days, and both Patrick and Outram regarded speeds in excess of 45 m.p.h. as being ungodly. Furthermore, tradition demanded a lengthy stop for breakfast at the George in Stamford, and a lengthier stop for lunch at either the Punch in Doncaster or else the Swan in Aberford. There was ample time to admire the bridge over the Trent designed by Kitson's great-uncle or to speculate in whimsical fashion over the ruins of 'Shapiro's New Horse Repository' in Doncaster. Grinding over Bowes Moor in third gear the journey began to seem interminable, but spirits lifted when we reached Penrith and even more when we reached Keswick. We would finally arrive in Borrowdale not long after 5.00 p.m., too late to secure a comfortable bed, perhaps, but in time for tea or beer before supper.

We hunted on foot over a limited area around Great Gable, and we hunted for each other rather than for lakes.

That is to say, we pursued two human hares, nominated afresh at breakfast each day and equipped with horns; by tooting these horns when they felt lonely the hares could engage the attention of any hounds in the vicinity. Wise hares offered themselves up for capture before lunch-time, somewhere on the slopes leading down into Ennerdale, leaving time for a walk over Haystacks to Buttermere and a swim in the lake, naked, before an enormous tea with apple pie and rum butter, served by Miss Nelson at Gatesgarth. Thus fortified, we would embark on the trek back over the Honister Pass to the food that Mrs Cockbain had ready for us at Seatoller – food that bore little resemblance to what the Trinity kitchens made of rations. And then, most evenings, we would gather by the light of a primus lamp around the out-of-tune piano, at which Outram really came to life, using ten fingers to play with and apparently ten others to flick up the keys which stuck. Most of the older members had a song which could be dragged out of them without too much difficulty. Mark Pryor, an entomologist of captivating charm and wit until a tragic road accident sent him into a coma which ended only with his death, is remembered by Lake Hunters for 'Villikins', and Patrick Duff for a tuneless rendering of 'Little Billee'. Walter's song was a mournful ditty, of which the refrain ran:

> The old baby farmer, the wicked Mrs Dyer,
> At the Old Bailey her wages is paid.
> In times long ago we'd 'a' built a great fyer
> And roasted so nicely that wicked old jade.

Not everyone who went on the Lake Hunt enjoyed it; some, indeed, were reputed to have slipped into Keswick by bus after the first day and to have sent themselves telegrams demanding their immediate return home to attend a grandmother's funeral. But I loved it, and I think that it played a significant part in turning me into the person that I now am. At the very least, it helped to shape my sense of humour.

91

The dons whom I first encountered at Trinity paid me little attention, those I got to know through the Lake Hunt made up for that with lavish hospitality. I owe to Patrick Duff my first taste of *foie gras*; to Mark Pryor my first and only experience of what it feels like to eat off silver plates; and to Walter my first taste of oysters. These were heady sensations in the grey years of post-war rationing. The oysters were served in a memorable party which Walter hosted in an upstairs room at the Pitt Club, an establishment of which he was probably Senior Treasurer at the time; it was a favourite venue for him and Outram Evennett and Kitson Clark for breakfast on Sundays. I also owe to Walter my first experience of the Western Highlands of Scotland, having spent a golden holiday as his guest in his rented house near Arisaig, together with Richard Adrian. We walked on the beaches there collecting cowrie shells, playing golf on the sporting Arisaig course, went sailing with his landlady's family, and read Scott and Doughty's *Travels through Arabia Deserta* after dinner. Later, we accompanied Walter on a remarkable visit to the Scottish home of another Fellow of Trinity, Steven Runciman, on the island of Eigg.

Walter's rooms in Trinity were on the first floor of the King's Hostel building, overlooking the bowling green. They communicated with the rooms occupied by Outram and, less directly, with those of Patrick Duff, and these two were liable to appear when Walter was dispensing coffee, beer and conversation after dinner. Patrick was at that time waiting to succeed to the chair of Roman Law. Outram was a historian, who would have preferred to be a concert pianist but had too nervous a temperament for that career; his performance of the Liszt piano concerto at a college concert was preceded by months of increasingly desperate practising, his pounding of a dumb keyboard being clearly audible next door. There were many other bachelor Fellows living in the College besides those I have mentioned, of course, plus two eccentric married ones who preferred their wives to be accommodated elsewhere. The married ones were Professor Hollond and Professor Besicovich. Harry Holland was a lawyer, who succeeded the historian Jim Butler as Vice-Master. He was notorious for his precise articulation, his 'secret' being, in his own words, 'to use the lips', and when he began a speech, at a College Meeting called to discuss a topic which concerned women in some way, with the phrase 'I am a married man, although a semi-detached one', the effect was telling. His wife Marjorie was a Fellow of Girton and lived there until they both retired and set up house together in Madingley Road. Professor Besicovich was yet another brilliant mathematician, a Russian emigré who was reputed to lock his Russian wife into his New Court room while he himself dined at the High Table. Of the genuine bachelors, the ones who had most in common with Walter were probably Professor Andrew Gow, a crusty and disconcerting Classical scholar with a soft centre, who had once, like Walter, taught at Eton, and Professor Donald Robertson, another Classical scholar who was soft outside as well as in. There were also Professor Denis Robertson and Piero Sraffa, both economists; Binnie, an engineer; the Reverend F. A. Simpson, Kitson Clark, Michal Vyvyan and Jack Gallagher, four more historians; and several others besides. All these I got to know when I became a Research Fellow myself in 1950. Most of them went out of their way to be kind to me in various ways, and I spent three happy years playing bowls with them, but by then Walter had moved on.

In Walter's sitting-room there were sofas and easy chairs which must have followed him from Eton, covered in white hessian with green piping; he was extremely proud of this combination, having designed it for himself. When he moved on he gave me one of the sofas, a particularly derelict and sagging specimen which I promptly had re-seated. It was never half as comfortable again, but it served me well until

Walter reclaimed it, still clad in whitish hessian, almost 20 years later. Just how many evenings I spent sitting on it before it ever came to me I am unable now to estimate, but several of them are still clear in my memory, as are the stories and aphorisms which Walter dispensed with characteristic and infectious enthusiasm. A short selection of the latter will immediately bring him to the mind of anyone who knew him.

> There are three essential principles in life: never write to the newspapers; never marry a widow; above all, never do anything for the first time.

> The poet who is supposed to have written about warming 'both hands before the fire of life' has been misinterpreted. His word was 'hams' not 'hands'.

> Simpson has spent the whole war in gathering honey, and now he has so much stored in his room he does not know what to do with it. I tell him that he should use it to get himself *embalmed*.

I cannot think of such sayings without seeing Walter looking over his spectacles with an owlish gaze to gauge his auditor's reactions, and without hearing him titter.

I remember him picking off his shelves one evening a well-thumbed copy of one of Kitson's books, and entertaining us by reading passages from it. Kitson was a learned, conscientious, and exceptionally kind man, who did not at all deserve mockery. He tended to attract it from contemporaries such as Walter, however, though it was affectionate mockery rather than the barbed variety which was directed, with full justification, at Simpson. Kitson was mocked for his girth, and for the agony he experienced during prose composition – so intense, it was said, that his bellowings of despair could be heard all over the Great Court. Out of his midnight labour came some splendid flourishes:

> As in a boxing match, when the assailants rest from their labours and the air is filled with the flapping of towels, so . . .

94

It was the hour before dawn, when the mind is assailed by ghosts and hampered by embryos.

These we giggled at with Walter when he read them, and we giggled at the sonnet composed by one of his pupils, of which the best line was felt to be: 'The father toils the bacon to bring home.' I tried to write a sonnet myself after that and showed it to Walter, but his only comment was: 'The enjambment is imperfect'. He was, of course, a schoolmaster at heart.

There was a dark side to Walter at that time. He could be morose as well as lively, and he shared this mood too with his younger friends. In retrospect, it is clear to me that he was far from certain what he was doing at Trinity after the war and whether he should stay there. He evinced little enthusiasm for a future devoted entirely to classical scholarship and little conviction that the flash of inspiration which, according to his version, had won him his fellowship before the war would ever be repeated. He was over forty, marking time in an environment which was congenial but which, despite post-war shortages, offered too much comfort and too few challenges.

The news that he was moving to Westminster as headmaster, and exchanging his cosy bachelor life for the adventure of marriage stunned us all. He must have known very well, however, that it was in these new directions that his best chance of real happiness and fulfilment lay.

The following article appeared in the
Evening Standard *on Friday, 9 December, 1955*

WESTMINSTER HEAD
HAS THAT MAX MILLER LOOK

There is nothing of the Minor Prophet in the appearance of Mr Walter Hamilton, headmaster of Westminster School. But the man who found a don's life too easy is a teacher in the great tradition. Mr Walter Hamilton, the headmaster of Westminster School, does not look at all the sort of head whose unexpected appearance freezes the rioting Fifth into silent immobility. He is not tall, white-haired, eagle-eyed, lantern jawed. He is of medium height, rising 48, has a suspicion of podginess. Something in his eye suggests Max Miller rather than a Minor Prophet.

Faced with a schoolboy riot he would probably organise it into a discussion group – with himself in the chair.

Notwithstanding his appearance, he can be severe, they say. 'It's not what he says, it's the way he *looks* at you,' a pupil testifies.

Hamilton is a headmaster in the old Humane tradition. That is, he is a scholar and a teacher.

Nowadays a majority of headmasters are primarily administrators, who teach only nominally. And increasingly they are financial experts; men whose talents resemble Mr Clore's or Mr Wolfson's rather than Colet's or Ascham's, and who never take a class themselves. 'I don't believe that's right,' says Hamilton.

He himself is a high authority on the ancient Greek philosophers, and he enjoys instructing the young.

Westminster is perhaps the foremost school in London. In

96

the early and middle eighteenth century it was incontestably the most aristocratic school in England.

Today it has 190 boarders who pay £310 a year and 190 day-boys at £170. There is an endowed foundation of 40 resident Queen's Scholars – the Queen being Elizabeth I.

Its present headmaster owes his high position, he will tell you, to a series of accidents. A brilliant classical scholar, he became a fellow of Trinity College, Cambridge, when he was 23.

A bright young don, the comforts of Combination Room about him, the satisfaction of a lifetime's work on the Greek philosophers before him, there he might have stayed.

Then in 1933 four Eton masters were killed climbing in the Alps. Replacements were needed with urgency, and someone talked Hamilton into going – temporarily of course.

Hamilton was not himself a product of one of the great public schools. He was educated at a modest grammar school, St Dunstan's, Catford.

He was to start teaching at a school where a large proportion of the staff were old boys; whose two brands of football were played nowhere else in the world; whose pupils had developed the art of being supercilious to a quite exquisite pitch. But schoolboys in the mass – like private soldiers – are good judges of character. Hamilton was a success.

Not a Denis Compton or a C. B. Fry, he played games with a mixture of earnestness and buffoonery, as if to say: 'I know I look silly, but what of it?' The boys found him sympathetic.

They imitated his voice. They are still imitating it. It is a good voice to imitate. It is low, deep, melancholy and yet nasal. He could dub a depressed blood-hound for a cartoon film admirably.

He resigned his Cambridge fellowship. In his fourth year at Eton he was appointed Master in College – housemaster of the 70-odd King's Scholars, the intellectual élite of the school.

97

In 1946, after nine years as a housemaster, he resumed his fellowship at Trinity. 'They suddenly asked me back. Quite unexpectedly. I felt I was getting into a rut at Eton, so I accepted.'

He was appointed University Lecturer in Classics and, very soon, tutor of his college.

At Eton he had been a diffident man. Typically, his favourite poet, whom he was much given to quoting, was A. E. Housman.

Housman was a shy, ascetic, classical scholar. His pagan pessimism has been aptly summarised by Ezra Pound: 'Woe, woe, woe. We shall soon all be dead. Therefore let us behave as if we were dead already.'

Hamilton's second stay at Cambridge showed much more the influence of – say – Byron. He went about and met people. He found undergraduates appreciated his dry, sly humour. He became a leading light of the Pitt Club, which, despite its name, is social, not political; the 'smart' club for the undergraduate to belong to.

And he wooed and won the outstandingly pretty sister of a boy who had been in his house.

She was 21 years younger than he; they have lived happily ever after, and have two sons.

In 1950, again quite unexpectedly, he was offered the headmastership of Westminster. He had intended to spend the rest of his life at Cambridge, and he felt inclined to refuse.

Friends talked him out of it.

Westminster and marriage have seen Hamilton positively blossom. His translation of Plato's Symposium in a paperbacked series has so far sold 70,000 copies.

This year he has been elected chairman of the Headmasters' Conference. This body is composed of the headmasters of independent schools of a certain standing.

It is an honour which gives him much pride. He feels it is the answer to people who say he is no administrator.

He is a Governor of the London School of Economics. 'I can't think why I was appointed,' he says. 'I know nothing about economics. Fortunately our duties are nominal.'

He is also chairman of the Children's Advisory Committee to the ITA. His attitude to television admirably demonstrates his old-fashioned outlook.

'When Sir Kenneth Clark asked me to join the committee I said I didn't mind, but as I didn't own a machine (he meant a set), and had no intention of acquiring one, I didn't see what use I could be to him. I didn't realise I was to be flattered with the chair. I suppose a schoolmaster imparts an aura of respectability ... Anyhow they sent a machine along. It's not clear whether it's given or lent.

'The ITA is compelled by law to take our advice. But as we can only complain after the programme, it is shutting the stable door after the horse is loose. In any case, I think television is bad for children except in very small doses.'

As to his spare time activities: he claims that during term he has no spare time – literally. During the long holidays he and his family migrate to the island of Mull in the Hebrides.

There he has bought a house – purely by chance again. He was on his way to see another house, when he noticed a white-coated stone house for sale ... chose Mull because being less spectacular than Skye, for instance, there are fewer tourists.

The life of a don at Oxford or Cambridge seems to me to be one of the pleasantest existence can offer. And the life of a schoolmaster almost equally unpleasant.

Hamilton's hopping from one to another and back seems curious. 'A don's life is too easy' he explains himself. 'Undergraduates are what they are. You cannot mould them. Unless you are passionately interested in the minutiae of classical research, the life is unsatisfying.

'I expect I shall stay at Westminster until I retire. That is, I shan't go out of my way to move. I have never planned any of my moves ...'

6

WESTMINSTER

Headmaster 1950–57

Stephen Lushington

A FTER THE WAR, when Walter had returned to Trinity as
Fellow and Tutor, I wrote to ask his advice as to whether
I should apply to teach at Eton; I was, briefly, disappointed
when he discouraged me. I went to teach at Westminster
School instead under John Christie, a most delightful man,
always ready for an interesting conversation on literature or
the theatre. Two years later I was very sorry to hear that he
was leaving to become Principal of Jesus College, Oxford;
but events were to take a happy turn. One day he took me
aside and said, 'A friend of yours is going to be the next Head
Master.'

Walter's appointment to Westminster established his
remarkable career in schools for the next sixteen years. As I discovered years later, when I became one, a headmaster's position
is a lonely life, since members of staff rarely speak out to him as
they would to colleagues. However, if you were old friends before
such a difference of status is involved, there is a certain ease and
comfort, which I hope Walter felt as much as I did.

At the time this did not make me a particularly good judge
of Walter's problems and difficulties, failures and successes,
or ultimately of his achievements as Head Master. What
follows owes much to hindsight, not only mine but that of
staff colleagues and old boys, and also takes into account
articles in the School magazine, *The Elizabethan*, and
contemporary letters from boys, parents and governors.

Walter was by no means confident when beginning his first headmastership. And Robert Birley wrote, reminding him of the note he passed him at his first masters' meeting at Eton: 'I wish I could repeat the same message, but of headmastering it would not be true!' However, he had a flying start, for he was a fine scholar, with a gift for administration, and the ability to get on with people; and he was already respected for his judgement, and for his integrity of character. It is notable how often the word 'wisdom' came to be used about him in later correspondence.

What of the problems he found awaiting him in Dean's Yard? Loneliness, perhaps, came first; a cavernous top-floor flat, and his new position, none of the 'clubbableness' of Cambridge; nor – as in College at Eton and later at Rugby – a house full of boys around him. The outgoing friendliness and helpful attitude of John Carleton, Second Master and Master of the Queen's Scholars, meant a great deal to him. He wrote to his old friend, James Duff, 'The staff are very welcoming, and my Under Master is a particularly congenial man, a bachelor of my own age, with whom I think I shall have no difficulty in becoming intimate. This is a great piece of good luck, because I do miss the more intimate atmosphere of Trinity.'

Of incomparably greater importance, however, was to be the change in Walter's personal life. In October 1950 he announced his engagement to Jane Burrows, the sister of one of his old pupils in College at Eton. Very few people knew of it in advance and, when the news broke, he was inundated with letters of congratulation from friends, parents of boys and old pupils, all expressing their delighted surprise and happiness for him. Only one writer volunteered her husband's doubts who thought it was rash to marry someone so much younger than himself – she was nineteen and he forty-two. Whether it was rash or not (and Walter always enjoyed doing the unexpected) their marriage could not have been a happier or more successful one. They were married in King Henry VII's Chapel in Westminster Abbey on 31 March 1951. One old friend and pupil wrote to Jane after Walter had died, 'I think all his friends noticed – I certainly did – how the spells of gloom seemed to be reduced to almost minuscule size by comparison, after he had found you. You obviously gave him wonderful happiness, security and contentment, which was enhanced by your family. What a tremendously fulfilling life he had.' Walter would have wholeheartedly agreed.

Another important factor in Walter's life was that he inherited from his predecessor an extremely efficient and congenial secretary, named Anne Morse. She did *The Times* crossword puzzle and she laughed at his jokes. She had worked for John Christie for a year or so before Walter arrived and she found Walter was on the whole more relaxed and accessible to boys and staff. He had a relaxed style of dictating too. This had its drawbacks because he was frequently very difficult to hear. He would walk up and down his large study, pipe in mouth, talking through the pipe stem with teeth clenched, often turning his back, perhaps to look out of the window. However, as he liked to pause frequently while he dictated to exchange glances of understanding and the odd joke, it was possible to get him to repeat what he had said, which he never minded doing.

He also differed from his predecessor in being newly married. The Head Master's flat was immediately above the study and Walter would frequently go up to see if Jane was all right. He was very conscious that she might be lonely. In any case, being a Head Master's wife is another lonely position, all the more so for one a good deal younger than most of the Westminster wives. It was also very strange for Jane, who found herself, as the Head Master's wife, entertaining boys in the School to dinner, who were only a year younger than she was. History doesn't relate how the boys found it.

Abbey – Boys – Buildings – Scholarship – Staff: these might be thought of as the hand of five cards dealt the new Head Master, and an unpromising one at that.

Most public schools are an independent domain, ruled by the headmaster, assisted or impeded by a bursar, and visited three or four times a year by a Governing Body, whose chairman may often act as a valuable consultant. There are usually ample playing-fields, and space for building and expansion when funds are available.

At Westminster things are different. The Dean is chairman of the Governing Body, and two of the Canons are also likely to be members. The School has the 'privilege' of worshipping in the Abbey at times and under conditions approved by the Dean. There was more than one 'row': when, for instance, Walter had altered the time of the School's short morning service by fifteen minutes, one of the Canons felt he had not been consulted, and stalked through the Abbey in the middle of it. The only playing-field within easy reach is several minutes away at Vincent Square. Any land or buildings not owned by the School are owned by the Abbey. The price of central London property is prohibitive.

The Abbey then consisted of mostly elderly resident clergymen who expected the calm of a Cathedral Close; the School consisted of several hundred young people, many of them also residents, who liked to make a cheerful noise. It was not always a harmonious mixture.

In Walter's time an extremely Trollopian situation prevailed. One particular Canon who occupied No 20 Dean's Yard (the most vulnerable house) and was also Rector of St Margaret's, found that the noise, especially on Cadet Corps parade days, impeded the construction of his sermons, and wrote tiresome and irritating letters of complaint on this and other matters to the Head Master, whose diplomatic skills were much exercised – and developed – over several years. One thing emerges clearly from the voluminous

103

correspondence, that Walter's patience (in public at least) never flagged and that the Canon in question came to appreciate this and to respect Walter's efforts to deal with his complaints. It was perhaps not surprising that when the Abbey was closed for the Coronation, and in spite of preliminary overtures on both sides, Walter decided that the School would not use St Margaret's for its services, but St Matthew's, Great Peter Street.

During the War years the School had been evacuated to three different places one after the other, and the effort and organisation needed to keep it going in makeshift accommodation in the depths of the country were enormous. The School returned home, reduced to only 135 boys, and to find some of the most important buildings bombed and unusable and much of the rest in considerable disrepair. Very much of the credit for the school's survival goes to John Christie, but his great efforts had taken their toll, and it was not surprising that Walter encountered problems of discipline and morale, as well as acute structural and therefore also financial ones.

He found some of the boys 'too clever' and 'arrogant', and his early attempts to deal with senior boys were not always successful. It was a mistake to impose what were in fact Eton customs (and soon discovered to be so) on Westminster boys – it hurt their pride and sense of independence. So the idea of 'capping Beaks', i.e. putting up a finger to acknowledge a member of staff when passing, soon lapsed. Coloured waistcoats and other ornaments for School Monitors survived, but with muted approval. The idea of improving manners and self-respect took time to bear fruit.

Walter was much liked by individual boys, who responded to his fair treatment and personal interest. He treated senior boys as adults, much as a university don would treat undergraduates. One boy was caught climbing over the Abbey roof at night, another wrote an answer off his own bat to a letter in the *Church Times* from the rector of St Margaret's. Both actions put the Head Master in an awkward position with the Governors, but Walter bore the brunt, and did not take it out on the boys.

Walter's teaching was quietly appreciated, though it had none of the vibrant enthusiasm of John Christie's. There are several letters of thanks from Oxford and Cambridge OWs whom he had taught. David Lloyd Jacob wrote from Christ Church, 'I know that those of us who were taught by you felt that we were the recipients of a great privilege. It was something I would have been sorry to have missed.' Hubert Picarda wrote, 'Walter was a very fine and extremely gifted communicator, and I remember this through his teaching of Latin verse.'

Thomas Pearce, now on the staff of the Classics Department at the University of Aberdeen, writes: 'As a teacher he was especially concerned with the importance of basic grammatical and linguistic knowledge'; he believed that 'without a good foundation an attractive superstructure was of dubious value. This provided a contrast and a complement to the more imaginative and adventurous approach of Theo Zinn.' The letter goes on: 'I can say now that many years of attempting to teach Classics myself have deepened my appreciation of Walter's approach.'

There were those who found Walter's teaching dry – but the class was always liable to be enlivened by humour. On one occasion, when a boy blundered while translating, there was at that moment a clap of thunder and a storm of rain. 'Oh Renshaw,' cried Walter, 'the heavens weep!' On another, when much building was going on around Dean's Yard and Little Dean's Yard, and steam-hammers and road-drills were painfully disruptive, Walter was taking the Classical VIIth. The noise stopped and for a few blessed minutes all was quiet. Suddenly a face appeared at the classroom window – Wilby, the Clerk of the Works, at the top of a ladder, had come to mend the sash-cord. 'Oh!' cried Walter at this final straw, 'I am a Job among schoolmasters!'

Meanwhile, his academic reputation was growing: it was while he was at Westminster that Penguin Classics published the first of his three translations of Plato, *The Symposium*. In the bibliography of his edition of *The Symposium*, Sir Kenneth Dover wrote, 'The translation of Walter Hamilton is more perceptive and felicitous than those of Benjamin Jowett and W. R. M. Lamb; it is also closer to the Greek than that of Michael Joyce.' By 1990 it had been republished twenty-nine times.

When teaching, his feeling for words and clarity of expression, in good plain English, never left him. Andrew Roberts, now Professor of the History of Africa at the School of Oriental and African Studies, wrote in a letter of 25 August 1990 about his last term at Westminster (1955):

After the History Seventh had worked its way into Oxbridge, Walter generously invited us to an informal weekly class in English. By then, my prose style was tiresomely baroque: Walter, with proper Socratic guile, introduced himself as a simple fellow who didn't know much about Lit. Crit. and would probably fail to spot our allusions, so could we keep our writing crisp and clear? It occurs to me now that – inverting Ezra Pound – Walter was in effect suggesting that prose should be at least as well written as poetry. Certainly, it was his delight in verse by Housman and Samuel Johnson which gave me most pause for thought, and as much as anything cured me of my worst Coleridgean convolutions. In Walter's reading of Johnson's lines on the death of Mr Robert Levet, even schoolboys could sense Latin and English joining together to register strong emotion:

> Yet still he fills affection's eye,
>   Obscurely wise and coarsely kind;
> Nor, lettered Arrogance, deny
>   Thy praise to merit unrefined

Walter's wisdom and merit were neither obscure nor unrefined, but in assuming such a character he showed himself a remarkable teacher.

It was a shrewd move on Walter's part to arrange a full visit of the School by His Majesty's Inspectors during his second term. This not only enabled him to assess the teaching, but their Report also provided valuable 'ammunition' and support to his proposals for improving the buildings. Whether as a result of the inspection, or independently, or both, Walter considered that the staff he inherited were not all of the highest quality. By the time he left, both in terms of scholarship results and of the skill and character of the teaching staff, the situation had been transformed. In 1954, for example, Westminster gained a higher percentage of awards to Oxford and Cambridge than any other school.

Staff opinions of Walter are more numerous, perceptive and varied than those of old boys. Francis Rawes says, 'He had an old-fashioned integrity. That's why we trusted him. He was honest, shrewd, and had no frills.' John Wilson wrote, 'Walter had powers of decision-making. People were given answers. There was no trace of deviousness about him, but he couldn't bear people who took themselves too seriously, or were pompous.' Walter was entirely free from conceit and self-importance, but he believed most firmly in the inviolable dignity of the office of Head Master. This conviction stood him in good stead both within and without the School. However, those members of the staff who were in trouble or difficulty, because of lack of money, family problems, or inadequate accommodation, found Walter patient, sensitive and determined to help. On one occasion he created a flat for the Prag family from the top floor of the Sanatorium, against much internal opposition. Another teacher complained of Walter's apparent lack of interest in staff members who were *not* in difficulties!

Walter was a fine selector of staff. One of his most inspired appointments, in fact the first and in his own field, Classics, was Theo Zinn, from Charterhouse and Oxford; Zinn felt his interview was a terrible anticlimax as Walter began, 'I don't

107

really know what to say to you' in his gloomiest tones. But it was not only towards Classics that Walter's efforts were directed. In Science, a subject neither familiar nor congenial to him, the School was faced with extremely restricted facilities, and no apparent room for expansion. Walter's first step was to appoint Geoffrey Foxcroft as Senior Physics Master, and give him a free hand to reorganise the teaching. Later, two years after leaving for Rugby, Walter was to invite Foxcroft to do the same job for Science there.

Geoffrey writes:

> When I took up the appointment in 1952 – more than a year after my interview – Walter simply said I was to get the department going again. There was not much to build on in 1952 – so much had disappeared after use of the labs by a government department – but Walter gave much support and found some money (£250 I think!) to make a start. He protected me in the early days when it was necessary to lift Science from the 'Woodwork' section of the timetable to the respectable part. And as results improved and the numbers wanting to do Science increased, he always said 'Well done my boy' – or at least let you know he had noticed.
>
> As Science expanded, the greater demands on timetable time inevitably caused the growth of opposition. Walter showed masterly tact in allowing much formal discussion. He was well aware that the growth was inevitable (I like to believe he thought it was desirable too) and he steered those discussions to the benefits of the sciences. The expansion resulted in the need for new laboratories (eventually funded by the national Industrial Fund), the design of which was left entirely to the scientists who were going to use them.

In the final tribute to Walter's headmastership *The Elizabethan* of August 1957 records, 'Before he left, he had carried out, often in the face of great difficulties, all the preparatory negotiations for the enlargement and reconstruction of the Science buildings.'

Walter was not an all-rounder. He understood the

importance to the School of a respectable level of success in games and their value to an individual boy's progress, but he was himself no self-confessed sports fan. He was a wonderful promoter of scholarship, but he was less culturally aware than Westminster had been accustomed to in their Head Masters. He was not musical himself, though he would have liked to have been, and left the running of music entirely to the Director of Music, at that time Arnold Foster. He attended school concerts, but on many occasions he found it difficult to contain his boredom. Towards the end of one oratorio he was overheard muttering, 'Oh dear! Oh dear! Look at all of them – Amen, Amen, Amen – they fill me with unutterable gloom.' Those who knew him well recognised this as not wholly serious; but it took most of the staff a while to appreciate Walter's tone of voice, and the way it reflected his sense of humour.

Certain ways in which he reacted to staff, provoking criticism, can also be traced back to his experience at Eton. His impatience with staff wrangles at meetings was perhaps due to the nature of 'Chambers' at Eton, where the daily mid-morning meeting of staff was merely a gathering of individuals with points to make to each other and a brief period of announcements by the Head Master. Similarly, there was a tragedy at Westminster when a boy died after running round Dean's Yard and the housemaster felt let down because Walter evidently expected *him* to let the parents know. During Walter's time as Master-in-College at Eton, there was no question of the Head Master informing any parent of a boy's death or serious illness – it was always the housemaster's job. But Walter was moved to tears when announcing what had happened.

Concerning parents, he was always ready to support a member of staff whose actions had been criticised. I recall one example from experience: on one occasion I had punished a day-boy for persistent lateness by making him come to school at 8 a.m. for a week. The father, a prominent old boy, protested that this didn't suit him and his wife, and demanded some alternative. I was afraid my letter rejecting this might seem rude, so I showed it to Walter. 'That's not nearly strong enough,' he said. So I wrote, 'I must ask you clearly to understand that I will not tolerate any interference in the discipline of my house.' Next day Walter received a furious telephone call from the father: 'I have had a most impertinent letter from one of your staff.' 'I know,' said Walter, 'I dictated it.'

Some contrasting views of Walter at that time are expressed by Theo Zinn, who was temperamentally Walter's opposite – brimming with enthusiasm, a devotee of music and culture, and much in need at that time of head-magisterial encouragement. He used to complain that the gloomy tones in which Walter said 'Good morning' depressed him for the day. Theo also felt keenly that the Head Master gave insufficient support to his post-war revival of the Latin plays. 'When I am shown the green light I go, and when it's red I stop; the yellow I find difficult.' He remembers, when he needed a vital member of the cast for the dress rehearsal, that Walter did not intervene to release him from a minor games commitment. However, the production of Terence's *Phormio* in Little Dean's Yard in front of Ashburnham House was a great success. Many later productions also owed much to Theo's enthusiasm, scholarship and inventiveness – but he continued to find Walter's temperament uncultured and irritating, and his teaching of Classics colourless (in contrast to his own).

During Walter's time I directed six school plays from *Hamlet* in 1950 to *The Cherry Orchard* in 1956, and his unobtrusive but benevolent support enabled me to rehearse at various 'awkward' times, including a full day's run through on CCF Field Days. I do not remember that Walter was himself enthusiastic about the plays, but being a different sort of egotist from Theo, I didn't mind!

An important Westminster tradition was resumed during Walter's time. In 1953 Election Dinner was revived after fourteen years. This summer evening occasion in College Hall, with historic silver on the table and distinguished guests present with staff and senior boys to listen to a Latin grace and Classical epigrams on set themes (for which in later years a translation was thoughtfully provided!), created an unforgettable atmosphere and reassurance that Westminster lived on as a distinguished school. Walter was most enthusiastic about these occasions.

Meanwhile the reconstruction of buildings and the expansion of the School were to a large extent interdependent. The restoration of College was completed in 1950 within a short time of Walter taking over as Head Master. King George VI came to open it. A letter to James Duff dated 7 May 1950 reads, 'I have spent most of today writing a speech for the King to deliver on 6 June, which I find peculiarly difficult. However, it is done, but perhaps he won't use it. I'm not looking forward to the affair at all, but no doubt it is all for the best that it should happen.' In fact the King did 'use it' and the 'affair' was a great success, although Walter never shared his successor's love of ceremonial and state occasions. On this occasion Walter paid generous tribute to John Christie, who afterwards wrote a warm letter of appreciation. Letters between them show that this good feeling lasted throughout Walter's time at Westminster.

In another, to Jane, four days after the royal visit, Walter wrote:

Everything went off without a hitch and people seem to think that it was really a great success. Both King and Queen were most friendly. Most of his speech was by me, but his jokes were his own and he delivered them well. I *did* have some trousers on (the Collegiate Body, of which Walter as Head Master and John Carleton as Under Master were members, wore red full-length cassocks). At one point the King remarked that I must be very hot and asked if I had. I replied that as I knew I had to sit on a platform I had thought it better to put some on . . .

I hope all this will have done the School some good, because I'm afraid it needs it. There really are some horrible problems. The organisation is slack and the boys rather casual, and I'm not at all sure that we shall be able to keep going financially. Also the staff isn't paid enough.

I met Princess Margaret at a sherry party at Trinity on Saturday and had quite a long chat with her, thus rounding off my royal week. She told me she couldn't understand how I could leave Trinity for Westminster, and I find it difficult to explain myself.

Walter doesn't say in his letter, adds Jane, that he had apparently opened his conversation with Princess Margaret by saying, 'I saw your father last week. He asked me if I'd got any trousers on.' He had met her and Princess Elizabeth at Eton several times so it was not quite such a bold remark as it may sound.

The ground floor of the now restored College building was used for a newly created day-boy house and christened 'Wren's'. The two day-boy houses of Ashburnham and Home Boarders had been merged when the numbers went down, and now there were some protests when Home Boarders was renamed. As Wren's first housemaster, I preferred the new name. This was not a Westminster point of view!

By the spring of 1951 the numbers had risen to 350, there being space for the increase. The School's income was much increased. Meanwhile, *The Elizabethan*'s leading article was called 'The Aftermath of War – Changes and Problems'. After alluding to the wartime emphasis on co-operation it goes on: 'But now in a larger and more unwieldy School the emphasis is more on obedience than co-operation. Westminster has always had the tradition of encouraging the individual and the balance has to be found between this and a well-disciplined establishment. The old order is disappearing. What is to come?' Walter had six more years which were to prove these anxieties needless; the discipline noticeably improved, but the scope for individuality remained.

The Busby Library (where the Classical VIIth was taught) and the classroom opposite were ready for use in the same year. In November 1952 Walter moved the Under School out of Dean's Yard to new premises in Eccleston Square. Pat Campbell, Walter's new appointee as Master, was to lay a foundation of good discipline and good manners as well as good teaching, which were to serve the entry to the main school for years to come.

In July 1953 the rebuilding of Grant's was completed. The private side, with its eighteenth-century façade on to Little Dean's Yard, remained intact, but the boys' accommodation, which had been described in the Inspectors' report of 1950 as 'constituting one of the worst boarding houses in the country', was entirely redesigned with study-bedrooms and excellent facilities. Three years later Rigaud's, the next door boarding-house, was also to be improved, though on a smaller scale, and the day-boys in Ashburnham moved across to the west side of Dean's Yard next to the Choir School.

18 and 19 Dean's Yard, which had been used for so many different inhabitants while all these moves took place, were at last 'free' and Walter decided to create a new boarding house to cater for the expanding demand. It was to be called 'Liddell's' after a Victorian Head Master who lived there from 1846. As Liddell's first housemaster I prefer to think of it named after his daughter Alice, who was born there and later became Lewis Carroll's Alice in Wonderland. It was over a hundred years before another child was born to a Head Master of Westminster – Robert Hamilton in 1953.

The measure of Walter's efforts for reconstruction is well expressed in *The Elizabethan*'s farewell tribute. 'When he

113

arrived in 1950, much remained to be done and there was little money with which to do it. Slowly, by painstaking committee work and patient and persistent negotiation the Head Master overcame the difficulties of making bricks without straw.'

Looking back on his first headmastership, and the difficulties of post-war Westminster, how did Walter – and Jane – survive? In a letter to James Duff, of 11 September 1953, he wrote, 'I have been poking about Mull with my Bursar, and think that I have found a house there, eight miles from Tobermory, which would do well if we could get it.' It did. From 1954 onwards Walter, Jane and their children used to spend the holidays at their house, Ardbeg, in the village of Dervaig. My family was invited to join them on two or three occasions. The effort of transporting small children and their equipment from London to a Scottish island was considerable, but the rewards were great – space, simplicity, the sea near by – the perfect contrast to the problems of a great school in the heart of London. One of Walter's gifts was to be able to relax and to enjoy himself. On one occasion when a friend remarked that Mull was a long way from Westminster, Walter replied, 'Yes, so far that all I can hear of it is the grinding of axes.'

Walter's happy relationship with the Bursar provided him with much fun as well as an admirable business partner – their offices were next to each other and the Bursar also acted as Registrar, who controlled entries to the School. Colonel Humphrey St John Carruthers (yes, really) was a 'type' whom Walter could fully appreciate, in a way that he could not always feel personally comfortable with, for instance, Theo Zinn, another larger than life 'type'. He laughed at Humphrey, who took this, rightly, as a sign of affection. He had been an extremely successful Colonel in the *Gurkhas* and he never lost his military manner. He was always beautifully dressed and enjoyed wearing a monocle. He saw things in black and white and was very practical; so that when a party of Muslim boys were coming to visit the School he was reported to have asked, in all sincerity, 'Will they need any equipment?' He meant, of course, were they bringing prayer-mats or would he have to provide them? He was fiercely loyal to Walter whom he always referred to as 'Caesar'. They remained devoted to each other until the end of their lives. Jane remembers well the regular telephone calls which always began, 'Hello, old boy' from either end.

In 1955 Walter became Chairman of the Headmasters' Conference, being elected for two years. His colleagues on the Committee had quickly recognised his distinction and personality. A full-page article appeared in the *Evening Standard*, entitled 'Westminster's Head has that Max Miller look', and is quoted in full at the beginning of this chapter. The headline may have seemed facetious, but the text provides, entertainingly but seriously, an 'outside view' of Walter's achievements.

When in the following year the offer of Rugby came, Walter and Jane had little doubt they must accept. The opportunity to became headmaster of a second great school would further his career, and an opportunity to bring up their children in the country was one to be taken very seriously. Rugby would have space. The flat in Dean's Yard was not large enough for their growing family and there was no garden. The staff, however, were stunned by the announcement that Walter was deserting them for Rugby and there was a strong feeling of reproach. No Head Master of Westminster had moved to another school before. Especially for the housemasters it seemed a 'let down'.

However, it was certainly not a sense that all was completed which attracted Walter to change, so much as a feeling that the School's future would be better served by someone more particularly attached to both School and Abbey than he was. The quatercentury lay ahead, and with

115

it a large-scale Appeal in which the support and goodwill
of old boys, and of the Abbey, would play an important
part. This, and the attendant ceremonies and occasions
ahead, were not a congenial prospect to Walter, and he
knew that they would be to John Carleton who was widely
known and liked; he had only left Westminster once in his
life for a brief period during the War. There could be no
doubt of his great love of the whole Foundation which had
become his home.

It is unusual for a Head Master to be 'in' on the
appointment of his successor, but on this occasion Walter was
consulted by the Governing Body and several letters from
individual members almost urged him to recommend a
successor. He was not wrong in supposing that the
appointment of John Carleton would be a popular one with
Old Westminsters.

When the news of Walter's appointment to Rugby became
known, letters poured in from all over the country: from old
Eton colleagues, friends from Trinity, bishops and business-
men, headmasters by dozens, old Westminster pupils and
parents; all seemed delighted, and were only in doubt as to
whether Walter was to be congratulated upon Rugby, or
Rugby upon Walter. One postcard said simply
'Congratulations on the news! One cannot keep these
vigorous young optimists down' and a postscript at the end
of another letter: 'You'll never achieve your breakdown if
you allow yourself these changes of scene.' Someone had
once asked Walter if he was an optimist or a pessimist. To
their surprise he replied 'An optimist'. 'Why, then, do you
always seem so gloomy?' 'Because I know my optimism is not
justified.'

A notable feature of these letters was the very striking and
carefully expressed tributes from members of the Governing
Body. Walter had written a personal letter to each of them
with notice of his decision and reasons for having taken it.

Lord Davidson wrote:

> I would like you to know how sincere is the gratitude, which I
> and my friends feel towards you, for all you have done for the
> School since you came to Dean's Yard ... I am certain,
> knowing all the circumstances, that you have come to the right
> decision to go to Rugby. You leave Westminster infinitely
> stronger in every way than when you came; this result is largely
> due to yourself.

Roy Harrod wrote from Christ Church:

> Your Head Mastership has been a very notable epoch in the
> history of the School and I believe you have achieved a great
> deal in raising it to a higher level. I'm afraid you have had a
> good many afflictions to bear in one way or another. I hope you
> realise that your stalwart patience, and your tact and
> perseverance, have been observed and appreciated.

From Lord Rea:

> Far from reproach (for deserting Westminster for Rugby) we all
> owe you an immense debt of gratitude, for putting Westminster
> back into a position approaching its old eminence in the
> seventeenth century. What you have done is quite invaluable,
> and if the School continues to go forward, it will be due in a very
> large measure indeed to the Hamilton momentum.

Finally, from Alan Don, Old Rugbeian, Dean of
Westminster throughout Walter's time and Chairman of the
Governing Body:

> Your departure from Dean's Yard has deprived the Foundation
> of its most distinguished ornament and you and Jane have left
> us who remain a sense of bereavement.
> But as I am not writing an obituary notice, let me say simply
> that many besides myself will greatly miss you. It has been a real
> joy to see the School making headway under your leadership and
> it has been a happiness to me to work alongside you during the

117

past seven years. I know that I have sometimes tried your patience and have added to your worries – but these occasions will, I hope, fade into the background as you look back.

We all missed him.

7

RUGBY

Headmaster 1957–1966

James Hunt

'I AM IN difficulties over Walter Hamilton,' wrote a distinguished Old Rugbeian. 'Memories are often too fragile or precious to expose to the cold searchlight of pen on paper. What words can recapture the warmth and solidarity "tam cari capitis"? They can't of course, but a memoir is a memoir and they must do their best.'

When the time came for Sir Arthur fforde to retire, Sir Will Spens, chairman of governors of Rugby School, had no doubt in his mind but that the Head Master of Westminster was the only man of sufficient stature to succeed him. He put strong pressure on Walter to accept the appointment, and the friends whom Walter consulted were strongly in favour of Walter accepting it. Sir Robert Birley, at that time Head Master of Eton, wrote:

> I hope very much indeed that you will go there. It has a really high standard and tradition of work and scholarship and the great thing is that it has genuine intellectual standards. Arnold still counts for a great deal, which is in most ways no bad thing, but has certain drawbacks. There is always a danger of too much moral earnestness. I feel you would be good for the place. I think you would find that Rugby suited you, and you would suit it. I don't mean that you are a typical Rugbeian-like person. You are not. The danger at Rugby is that the place will become overwhelmed by Brummagem Midlands. It is saved by its standard of scholarship and real cultural tradition, and you would not only preserve these, you would raise them. And it *does*

need someone who can see that it is liable to be ridiculous when, as I say, it becomes too morally earnest and I think you would see that all right.

And Walter did. Sir Robert, himself an Old Rugbeian, knew his Rugby; and fortunately for Rugby, Walter, having married comparatively late in life, had a young family and did not want his children to be brought up in the confines of Dean's Yard. So he accepted the appointment, which in the eyes of Rugby spelt promotion, but in Westminster's was regarded as 'decline and fall'. No previous Head Master had ever left to become headmaster of another school. A friend wrote: 'Dear Walter, I must congratulate you on your translation – if indeed it be promotion to leave the precincts of a palace for a railway station.' On the other hand a Trinity friend understood the appointment's significance: 'I am delighted and, speaking as an Old Rugbeian, I am particularly delighted that for the first time for a quarter of a century they have appointed a man who is not an Old Rugbeian. In fact it must be the first time they have appointed the *right man* since Arnold.'

For Walter it came as a cultural shock. As an undergraduate and later a tutor of Trinity College, Cambridge, a housemaster at Eton and a Head Master in the precincts of Westminster Abbey, he now found himself in an undistinguished Midland town in charge of a school of which the predominant buildings were Butterfield's. Nor was the tone of life at the school superficially to his liking. At the end of the eighteenth century Rugby could be regarded as the Eton of the Midlands and the North. Dr Arnold's *bête noire* had been 'privilege without responsibility' and his sympathies lay with working-men's clubs and the rising middle classes, not with the landed gentry of Warwickshire and Northamptonshire. There was also among the staff a group of earnest, if admirable, masters of an evangelical, and even Buchmanite, persuasion. Walter missed the lighter touch of his earlier experiences. But if Rugby at that time was not tailor-made to suit Walter, he was without any doubt the right man for Rugby.

On his arrival however the school showed itself formidably conservative and the new headmaster was quickly greeted with such slogans as 'Go back to Westminster, Wally'. The chapel lectern stood in the centre of the School Close wreathed in toilet paper to greet the eyes of masters and boys on their way to morning chapel. Walter's 'I won't have it' was enough to convince the school assembled in Temple Speech Room that what Walter wanted went. And again at the weekly chapel practice, at which behaviour had been notoriously bad, there was an occasion when the hymn-books were banged shut in concerted unison. Walter's roar shocked seven hundred boys into stunned silence.

His reaction to indiscipline was nothing if not simple. The initial resistance of the school was short-lived. But at the end of a term shortly after his arrival three senior boys slipped out on the penultimate night and with spray-paint wrote in large letters along the wall of a rival house, which had scooped nearly all the athletic cups: 'Go home, you hoary old men!' Walter required a call-over early on the final morning of term, which the whole school and housemasters had to attend. But by then Walter had already won universal popularity and, after wishing everyone well for the holidays, a cheer raised the roof.

Walter's headmastership ran from 1957 to 1966 and it was a great disappointment to very many of us that he was not there to preside over the quatercentenary celebrations. During that time a fellow headmaster was reported as saying that Rugby under Walter became the best school in the country, and on an occasion when he was contemplating early retirement an ex-member of the Governing Body wrote, 'You command the respect and affection both of masters and boys to a degree that I honestly think cannot have been matched since Arnold.' It was of Sophocles that Matthew Arnold wrote: 'He saw life steadily and saw it whole', words quoted by Simon Burrows, the Bishop of Buckingham, in his address at the Memorial Service held for Walter in Rugby School Chapel, when a memorial plaque to him was dedicated. The Bishop took as his text the account of the 'mixed up' man among the tombs whose name was 'legion' and developed the theme that 'putting the different bits together was the whole aim of life', and ended: 'Walter Hamilton taught me the meaning of integrity.'

Walter immediately won the confidence of the staff by his transparent sincerity. A former house tutor of his describes how, when he had been to see him about one of his pupils, at the end of the interview Walter leant across his desk and said 'I do approve of you, John'. In the animal world it is called 'bonding' and his adored and adoring golden retrievers, Tango and her daughter Tessa, set the pattern. But it happened naturally with Walter in all his human relationships. That was the secret of his success: he saw to it that the right people were doing the right jobs, filled them with confidence and trusted them absolutely. They were no idle words when an ex-governor wrote that he inspired simultaneously affection and respect.

Directors of Music are not uncommonly temperamental, prickly and difficult to deal with. This is how Rugby's Director wrote of Walter in a letter of condolence after his death:

He was one of the few great men I have known, and for whom I had the deepest respect, admiration and affection. I shall never forget our first meeting: it was my interview with him before he offered me an appointment on the Rugby staff. I had been warned by a friend of his that when Walter turned his big eyes on me it would be something like having two car head-lamps beaming in my face. The simile was rather apt. What I had not been prepared for was the apparent levity of the occasion. It was quite unlike any interview I had ever had and his lack of solemnity might have made me wonder whether he was making a serious assessment of me. But I was later to learn that in these marvellously relaxed and sometimes hilarious moments he had probably come to know much more about me than any of my more earnest interviewers had ever done.

But there were the times too when he could present a very stern appearance. I remember playing a somewhat unfamiliar tune to a hymn on Ascension Day. Walter waited outside chapel and rounded on me with, 'You have ruined my Ascension Day!' I weakly protested that I had played the tune in the *Rugby School Hymn Book*, which was by Sir Sydney Nicholson, an Old Rugbeian. This failed to pacify him and he glared as he told me that he did not care who wrote it. Barely two minutes after this explosion he relaxed and I realised that I had been forgiven my innocent indiscretion. I knew too that the incident would be totally forgotten, as he never bore grudges.

Walter was always accessible. There were no fixed appointments; just a knock on his study door and, if he was free, he would welcome me and immediately give me his whole attention, though on one occasion he laid aside *The Times* Crossword saying, in characteristic manner, 'You have found me out.'

The simplicity and directness of such an imposing personality continued to surprise and delight. An English master described his interview with Walter when he came to be appointed. 'We went through the usual topics. He then took me to lunch at the Three Horse Shoes. I didn't find small talk easy, and I don't think he did. After a desultory five minutes' conversation he said, "Is there anything you would like to ask me?" I considered. "No, I don't think so," I replied. "Well," he said in his most lugubrious tone, "You'd better think of something. We haven't finished the soup yet."'

Walter's idiosyncracies only increased people's affection for him. One was the habit of laughing at his own jokes with a teetering self-satisfaction which made them more delightful.

Once, at a tutors' meeting in School House, one of the tutors was talking at great length about a boy's progress when Walter – the crossword never far from his mind – glanced across at the senior tutor and exclaimed triumphantly, 'Misogynist!' Yet no one doubted he had been listening attentively to the monologue.

Although he was uneasy with the arrangement in modern times by which the headmaster was also housemaster of School House, Walter could not help being a good housemaster. He had not been in office for a week when a boy remarked, 'You can feel his personality all over the house.' A tutor writes, 'Occupied as he was by the concerns of the school, governing bodies, HMC and all that, he always had more than enough time for the House. He would watch fire practices and cricket, listen to singing competitions, and attend house play rehearsals, each of them a test of tolerance and endurance. Above all he was concerned with the boys in his house as people.'

This is how some of them remember him:

He made friends with boys because he managed to enjoy the things they enjoyed. He contrived to show real pleasure at a house dance or a house play. He would lose himself in the tensions of a close finish of a cricket match, and always there were jokes and laughter.

'He entirely lacked the vanity of tyranny' is how a member of the House, now a fellow of Walter's own college, put it: 'Mirth' is an old fashioned word, but it clings to my memories of Walter Hamilton. We speak of faces 'beaming' and being 'wreathed in smiles'. Walter could bring such trite expressions to life. It is unlikely that Lewis Carroll had Walter in mind when he invented the wonderful word 'beamish', and I doubt whether many people ever associated Walter with the phrase 'a beamish boy'. Yet although literal boyhood was far behind him by the time I knew him, it seemed that there remained about him something boyish in all the most auspicious senses of the word.

No one who ever came within range of his chuckle could ever forget it. It could be unnerving, not least for newcomers. It must have been a September evening in 1961 that I was ushered into the private side of School House for the first time to meet Walter and Jane Hamilton. I had travelled by train with the Edinburgh contingent and there was another new boy with me. A mountainous bear of a man, as it then seemed to me, greeted the two of us with a beaming enquiry: Which of us was Scot? Or so it sounded. I had yet to learn about the beauty of the Greek dual voice, but it was with one voice that the two of us responded: 'I am, Sir.' So it was for the first time that I heard the unique sound of Walter Hamilton's mirth. It was not always easy to know what to do in response, since no one could possibly match the extraordinary noise. It certainly perplexed me that first time. And yet there was always a conspiratorial ring in it, which seemed to want you to share in the inmost chink of the jest. As one grew to know him better, one recognised the shyness within this explosiveness. On this first meeting perplexity gave way to relief, when it turned out that what Walter had wanted to know was which one of us sported the name of Scott. It was the other boy.

I neither expect nor hope to meet a better scowler. Again one thinks of expressions that seem less like figures of speech when given such flesh and blood by Walter. He could 'look like thunder' and he could seem to give literal force to the phrase 'a black look'. He was capable of great severity and he could certainly inspire fear and trembling. But he did not present a sharp edge to the world as a matter of course. On the contrary there was something reassuring about the absence of all angularity in his physical presence even – dare one say it even now, in the comfort of retrospect – comforting. He took no pleasure in his power to impress himself on others. This is why boys could receive his wrath without resentment.

In memories of these younger days at School House it is invariably in such primary colours that Walter appears, whether beaming in sunny benignity or growling and scowling in black mood. There are other less dramatic attitudes in which I recall him, seated on the dais in Hall looking down on the House at meals, head thrown back in severe reflection, then tilted forward for amused contemplation over his half-rimmed spectacles of some venial youthful fatuity. Or again I see him leaning sideways to offer a patient forgiving ear to the more or less trying addresses of nervous youths and, no less patiently, though perhaps less forgivingly, their more assured parents.

As a housemaster he trod well-beaten paths, not bothering to snoop or pry. He reposed great trust in the senior boys in the belief, I would guess, that what they gained from the experience of responsibility outweighed the risks of their abusing it. He was himself a man of great natural authority, but he wielded it with modesty and discretion, and he expected the boys to whom he entrusted it to learn from his example. But what I learned most from him, and for which I am most grateful, was his sense of comedy. Perhaps nothing is more difficult or more precious for the young than to be educated in understanding what to laugh at, not least of all themselves.

What remains with me as with so many others, is the extraordinary physical presence of the man whose study I entered: the ominous bulk of the body, the lugubriousness of the voice, that seemed to exude all the gloom of an Eeyore or a Glumpuddle; impressions instantly offset by the conspiratorial twinkle of the eyes. He seemed from the very first to know all about me and to be on my side.

However it was not only as a housemaster, but above all as a headmaster that Walter brought to Rugby a great wealth of experience. He brought an open mind, a store of wisdom and an ability to foresee the logic of events. At his first Speech Day he said to the assembled school and parents:

No man in his senses could become headmaster of Rugby without a sense of his own inadequacy and apprehension; in my case that sense is magnified by the fact that I am a complete stranger following three headmasters who had Rugby in their blood and could therefore treat their audience on this occasion with a familiar intimacy that I dare not attempt. Many of you probably suspect me of harbouring revolutionary designs and are not likely to be reassured by professions of innocence. But

I can offer you more solid comfort. Believe me, the amount of harm (or good) that an individual headmaster can do to a place like this is strictly limited. A vast and complex organisation like Rugby is like a battleship, which can, I am told, accomplish even a slight change of course only in a matter of miles.

Walter was a man who knew how to develop, adapt and control, and essentially make things work. Having introduced himself in that characteristically disarming way, he showed at once that he was a master mariner when it came to putting a little pressure on the tiller. He went on to say that he intended to increase the amount of Science taught in the middle part of the school, and to extend to three years the one-year course in Science which was all that was provided for non-scientists. He also proposed the provision of a Common Course of a year involving a 'sizeable dose' of Science for new scholars, so that they would not be faced with an almost blind choice between the humanities and the sciences on entry to the school. Pragmatist that he was, he appointed as Head of Science an experienced teacher from Westminster (and a pioneer in Nuffield Physics), whom he knew he could trust and who wrote on his appointment: 'The only discussions I remember having with Walter took place on a train from Euston. He asked me "to bring the department up to date and prepare for the teaching of Science throughout the lower school". He said he thought it would take about five years to get it right. It was up to me and he would give his full support. He encouraged me to make the study of Science as worth while as the study of Classics. He showed me how to deal with people and guided me in the running of a department, and I got the greatest of pleasure working with him. Walter Hamilton was the best of all the headmasters for whom I worked, and I worked for seven.'

Not only were individual masters helped by such counsel and guidance, but all the housemasters found discipline easier to enforce under his aegis. Partly to this end one of his simple and effective reforms reinforced the authority of the school prefects, the 'Levée'. It was Doctor Arnold's firm principle that the intelligent should exercise authority. The tradition still obtained and the head of the 'Upper Bench', the Classical Sixth, automatically became head of the school, and the heads of houses were likewise sixth-formers. Moreover the members of the Levée were formerly only distinguished by a special tie. Walter had them dressed in blue blazers and provided with a special room to assist their cohesion, and membership of the Levée no longer depended solely on academic achievement.

On Speech Day the Headmaster had his own way of describing the change:

> One small improvement has been made during the year [he said], which I think will have a significance out of all proportion to its magnitude. This is the provision of a home for the School Levée, which has languished hitherto in an apartment, which it would be charitable to call 'sordid', with the result that it has been absurdly difficult for the members to form themselves into any kind of corporate body. Now, largely owing to the initiative of one or two of their members, they have been provided with a sort of parlour discreetly raised above the ground to elude the prying eyes of the vulgar, in which they can meet both formally and informally in reasonable comfort. The building was opened by my wife at dead of night last December and the ceremony took the form customary in launching a ship. I believe that the opportunity which the Levée has now been given of becoming a more cohesive and integrated body will prove to be a factor of prime importance in the well-being of the school.

Walter's sermons were remarkable for their cogency and clarity. He detested religiosity, but when it came to a clear definition of the Christian Faith, there was no hedging or evasive ambiguity. They all illustrate this quality. On one Speech Day he took as his text a passage from Isaiah 40:6 'The grass withereth, the flower fadeth, but the word of our God shall stand for ever':

It is an unfortunate, but almost universal, characteristic of human nature to tend to be bored by what is perfectly familiar, even to think that what is new must be far better than what is old simply because it is new. That is why 'old-fashioned' is a word of contempt. If we apply it, as we often do, to the achievements of past generations in art or literature or even science, we shall probably be very silly: if we apply it to the eternal moral truths which constitute the work of God, we shall be destroying our own prospects of happiness here and hereafter. Never allow yourself to think or to say that such a statement as 'it is more blessed to give than to receive' is old-fashioned; it is universally and eternally true, and it no more is or can be old-fashioned than the multiplication table.

The last two words shine like a searchlight on his argument.

Again, on a Remembrance Day he took as his text, 'He that loveth his life shall lose it and he that hateth his life in this world shall keep it unto life eternal.'

The desire to live [he said] is the strongest of all desires that man possesses, and never so strong as in the days of man's youth and strength, so that even the most disillusioned of poets can write of the fallen,

> Life, to be sure is nothing much to lose,
> But young men think it is, and we were young.

Is there anything that we can set on the other side of the account? Only this: 'He that loveth his life shall lose it and he that hateth his life in this world shall keep it unto life eternal.' Many even of those who accept the message of Christianity find it hard to appropriate for themselves the comfort which is to be found in the last words of my text. 'Men fear death as children fear to go into the dark' and the faith of most of us is not sufficient to dispel that darkness. Christians on the whole are as apt as other people to allow death a power of which it is the chief triumph of their faith to have deprived them. For if Christianity is not a belief in the comparative unimportance of physical death and the survival of the human personality beyond the grave it is nothing. 'If in this life only we have hope in Christ,' says St Paul, 'we are of all men most miserable.'

Christianity is an otherwordly religion; it does not offer any exemption from pain or suffering or any prospect of the gradual progress of human life towards perfection; it affirms roundly that we are strangers and pilgrims on the earth and that our citizenship is in heaven, and unless we accept this description of man's condition, unless the Crucifixion is a prelude to the Resurrection, the only message to be drawn from the Gospel is a message of despair. The Christian may well say, though in a different sense from Housman: 'Life to be sure is nothing much to lose.' The nature of the eternal life which is found by those who hate their life in this world is hidden from us and we have little confidence in the efforts which man has made to pierce the veil. But that there is a better country, in which we may look to be reunited with those whom we love, is an essential and integral part of the faith of Christ, who bids us in the simple and moving words of the English Prayerbook, 'Not to be sorry as men without hope for them which sleep in him.'

It's so beautifully clear. Walter's gift for trenchant and succinct expression was essentially the child of his own mind, but it was coloured by his admiration for the pragmatic sense of his hero Samuel Johnson, and his delight in the classical levity of P. G. Wodehouse. A fine preacher himself, he always acknowledged the excellence of the sermons of the few really able preachers who visited the chapel. But he did not suffer the failures gladly. Of one sermon he had to sit through, he claimed to have been affected by 'boredom of cosmic proportions'. Of his second master's sermons he once said, 'If James wrote his sermons down, he might understand what they meant.' He finally came to the conclusion – or so he confided in one of his housemasters – that the only sermons he really enjoyed were his own. Another housemaster wrote, 'One Sunday a visiting preacher preached a bad sermon on the Labourers in the Vineyard. Walter was so incensed that he preached on the same text the following Sunday. I have forgotten just how the trade unions were dragged into the first sermon; Walter's however was memorable. He took up the point of differentials and the familiar cry, "It isn't fair!" and concluded:

But this much at least is clear. Our eternal destiny is not going to be determined by anything resembling our mean little notion of fairness. As Wordsworth put it in his sonnet on King's Chapel, 'High Heaven rejects the lore of nicely calculated less or more.'

Does our parable allow us to go any further than that? I think it does; at any rate there are two things that occur to me. The first is that although the first set of labourers have worked all day and the last only one hour, the last have at any rate worked for that hour – the master does not distribute his reward to those who have not worked at all. I take this to mean that God's gift of eternal life, a gift which is not to be thought of as being susceptible to degrees of less or more, cannot be made to those who have made no contribution to his work however small or late. But equally the parable makes it clear that it is not for us to judge the value of another's contribution: it is God who knows the secrets of our hearts, and it may be that he can detect a contribution where it is quite invisible to any human observer. My second point is this: there is a small but important difference between the first labourers and the others which it is easy to miss. The first labourers agreed with their employer for a penny a day – they made a contract with him which in due course was fulfilled on both sides. The later labourers made no contract at all: all that the master said to them was 'Go ye also into the vineyard and whatsoever is right I will give you.' They took their employer on trust – they had faith that he would do the right thing by them. Is it fanciful to detect behind this a difference of attitude which perhaps determines the more generous treatment which the later comers receive?

Any reader of Walter's sermons cannot fail to become aware of his inspired common sense that penetrated even spiritual truth. His wisdom always contained an element of earthiness in the best sense.

His advice to leavers was full of practical good sense. 'Don't take to whisky before you are forty; it is good to have something to fall back on' was one piece. That it was effective was demonstrated in the Scottish Highlands by a tough Old Rugbeian engineer, aged about thirty, who refused the offer of a glass of whisky, remembering Walter's advice. So many of his sayings commanded a wide currency and nearly all were marked by the same characteristic and nicely judged understatement. After he had left Rugby, and while being taken round School House to see the alterations, the bachelor housemaster asked him whether he was sorry to have left. Walter replied, 'Yes, but not intolerably so.'

As a teacher, Walter's wit and humour were legendary. One pupil wrote, 'His real feel for the subject came over in the sheer pleasure in which it communicated itself to his pupils, with humour never far from the surface. There were anecdotes and analogies and you remembered both them and the point which they made, the sure sign of a real teacher. Above all, the lessons were fun and two-way fun. It might be the world-weary, "I always knew it was a mistake to do *The Symposium* with the Upper Bench", when that collection of male-only adolescents protested "Oh no, sir! It's the best speech in the dialogue."'

A classical scholar writes:

We had the highest standards of classical scholarship held up to us and we were well aware that Walter Hamilton himself embodied them, but coupled reassuringly with a warmth, humanity and sense of humour. He had a subversive twinkle in his eye which was very appealing in the sometimes rather rarefied atmosphere in the Upper Bench. How refreshing it was when he confided in us that he had not read Kant's *Critique of Pure Reason* and did not feel an urgent need to do so. We all respected him enormously, and not just because he flattered us by saying how much he preferred teaching schoolboys to undergraduates. 'Undergraduates are so silly!' he would say.

Another classic writes:

Walter's choice of language, his epigrams and sense of the absurd were all formidable and his enjoyment of his own wit, unlike men who have to strive more self-consciously for effect, managed to be engaging. The sly look at you over the half-spectacles and the high-pitched noise, which wasn't quite Ho! Ho! added to the humour rather than detracted from it.

Walter also taught English and the senior English master writes:

> It was my invidious task to enquire about or, at the worst, advise upon the authors he taught in that inferior medium. Most favoured were Dostoevsky, Dr Johnson, and of course, Keats. (The last two seem odd companions but the great W. J. Bate made the same pairing in his lectures at Harvard for upwards of twenty-five years.) On one unhappy occasion I suggested that he might substitute Shelley for Keats. It was foolish advice, for I should have known Shelley would prove wholly unsympathetic, both as poet and man – he lacked 'a bottom of good sense'. But the headmaster was one of the very few, if the only master, whose lessons were talked about during lunch, and it became apparent from such conversations that Walter had left his pupils more enlightened by disliking Shelley than a professional could have done by expatiating on his merits.

But Walter's dislikes often proved salutary. He was a man with strong convictions, and when challenged by someone who doubted or questioned what he said, especially if it injured his pride, he could be angrier than most. Not that his wrath, though formidable, lasted long, and nearly always it focused on some aspect of human nature rather than on the person. His was a righteous anger which did not make enemies. Even so, his devoted secretary saw none of this. For her he was 'the kindest of men' and never really angry, unless – as she puts it – with himself. However she does recall Walter coming from a vexatious masters' meeting and saying to her 'This would be a wonderful school if we only had boys in it.'

As a chairman he was able to guide a committee to a decision without cutting short the expression of opinion, and he was always fair. A housemaster writes:

> I'm not sure that he much enjoyed committees or housemasters' meetings. He did not add to their number. Over an awkward matter he could begin (deliberately) by hesitating, 'I think it

would be best if . . .' and then stop, looking over his half-moon glasses and then rephrase the personal view as a public pronouncement: 'After careful consideration I have decided . . .' Or, on his way to the staff room, 'What shall we do about this James?' And, almost in the same breath, he would open the meeting with 'After long and careful consideration I have decided that . . .' No one made any comment; one couldn't. He knew the difference between moments for consultation and moments of decision.

The effect of Walter's personality on the school at large is best described by one of his heads of school, who later took Orders, and had enjoyed a six-month friendship with him, which he treasured ever after:

This was when I began to perceive his massive competence. He knew what ought to be done. He tactfully guided me personally and extricated me from all kinds of foolishness. He knew how to cope with problems which are trivial enough no doubt, but which unsolved produce irritating pustules in the body of the school. But also with Walter one breathed the air of a wider world. There was always a distinct whiff of the Athenaeum; he seemed to know all the great and good and had taught most of them. He made us aware of a real world of power and decisions out there waiting for us to conquer. However it would be a complete mistake to think that his mind was not on running Rugby. It was just that his intelligence and energy of mind enabled him to sort out problems very quickly. It would have been easy for him to make an eighteen-year-old feel small. Nothing would have been less like Walter.

The other great quality I remember was his human sympathy. Whoever you were he was interested and attentive, not condescending or patronising. He made friends with boys because he managed to enjoy the things we enjoyed. He succeeded in finding genuine points of sympathy with a very high proportion of the people at Rugby.

And what of his influence on the school during the two years I was under him? He imposed his authority on the school because he was very professional and because he was extremely good at being in charge. He simply knew what to do. Discipline was better managed and everyone felt happier. I would guess that the ideal motivating him was intellectual rather than religious or political. If people thought right they would come to right decisions and lead good and useful lives. That is not to belittle his Christianity. I treasure the memory of his presence at 8 a.m. Holy Communion. It was voluntary for him as it was for us and he never looked as if he was there for any other reason than the rest of us – because he wanted to be. He also reminded us in his sermons that this area of life, like any other, needed intelligent and critical thought. I am told that public schools sometimes look to the 1950s as a Golden Age. If it was a Golden Age, then Walter Hamilton was a true Olympian in it.

But he was not motivated purely by an intellectual ideal and this is illustrated in one of his sermons, when he preached on the text, 'Be ye wise as serpents and harmless as doves.'

Although it is probably true that a bad man without intelligence will not be nearly so dangerous as he would be with it, I venture to suggest that it is equally true that without intelligence a good man will not be nearly so useful as he would be with it. This is the point I want to make, that it is perfectly possible to combine intelligence with innocence or goodness, the quality of the snake with the quality of the dove; that we have according to the words of the Gospel, a positive duty to cultivate whatever powers of intelligence God has given us, and we no more ought to neglect it than we ought to neglect the improvement of our moral character.

Walter's championship of intelligence is evident in everything he said or wrote. In his Guildford Lecture of 1970 on 'Education and the Search for Truth' he emphasised that 'the cultivation of the mind was a good thing in itself, the desire to set back by research what Housman called "the frontiers of knowledge", the hatred of nonsense and intellectual humbug, and above all the conviction that disputed questions could and ought to be settled by rational discussion. Without those things anything beyond purely utilitarian education would be impossible; they were vital to the survival of civilisation.' But for Walter there was more to education than the cultivation of the mind. In his farewell speech to the parents in July 1966 he made this plain:

> The time is coming – perhaps it has come already and we have no right to complain about it, when a Rugby education will cease to confer any particular advantage in the competition of life. What is left to make it an object of desire, worth obtaining even at considerable sacrifice? Rugby will remain desirable only because it is animated, however imperfectly, by certain principles and dedicated to the pursuit of certain ideals: ideals of truth and industry and loyalty and responsibility and self-control and concern for the welfare of others; because, in a word, it is a place of moral and religious as well as of mental education. But we have to recognise that this is not an easy position to maintain against the pressure of a secular world of dissolving values, and in particular, that it is idle to expect that Rugby can arouse in boys regard for these ideals if they are left to stand on their own when they are away from school against all the influences which pull in the opposite direction. This is the battle in which Rugby and schools like it are involved, and if there is any justification for continued existence then *we* have got to win it ...
>
> One last word: As I said earlier, the time has not yet come to say goodbye, but I cannot let pass the last opportunity I shall have of saying publicly how proud I am to be Headmaster of Rugby and how grateful for the kindness with which Rugby has treated me and my family. I am only too conscious of my many shortcomings. So no doubt are you, but when you reflect on them I would ask you to make the same allowance for me as Scott makes in *The Heart of Midlothian* for Jeanie Deans' husband: 'The man was mortal, and had been a schoolmaster.'

It would not be sufficient to close this appreciation without mention of Rugby's governing body in Walter's years. During his last term, one member wrote of his 'great financial and organisational ability' – a just description but somehow a bit 'professional' and not quite apt. Walter had inherited a highly professional Bursar, Philip Snow, brother of C. P. Snow, who had been a colonial administrator in Fiji, and he was quick to recognise his virtues. Philip on the other hand spoke of his Headmaster's 'masterly grasp of business detail' and how 'he disposed of paper work with impressive rapidity and thoroughness and lack of fuss'. The governors sat at a long table in the Jerusalem Chamber in Westminster Abbey, the Chairman and Deputy Chairman at the head and the Headmaster and the Bursar opposite each other to the right and left. 'This enabled me', Philip wrote, 'to see Walter's winks, when I needed encouraging, and also his almost imperceptible nods of the head, when he approved or disapproved of decisions being made as the meeting went on. He never said anything that did not need saying or could give a governor an opportunity to make a too unprofessional comment.' At governing body level too Walter relied on the right man in the right place.

But it was from the governors too that he did not always get the treatment he deserved. Early in his headmastership Sir Will Spens was succeeded as Chairman by Lord Cilcennin and he and Walter formed an ideal partnership which was unhappily cut short only too soon by Lord Cilcennin's death. Hubert Parker, a distinguished Old Rugbeian, would have been the perfect successor, had he not been appointed Lord Chief Justice. He accepted the chairmanship under strong pressure and against his better judgement, but found himself far too preoccupied to give either his time or his mind to the business of the school. So it came about that in the experience of his Bursar one of Walter's favourite expressions after governing body meetings was 'I am vexed'. In Philip Snow's own words:

> On one occasion a senior governor expressed concern over a set of examination results in Science and a need for strong improving measures. Next day was only one of two occasions when I saw Walter at a peak of vexation. 'How DARE he criticise the Science teaching' he exclaimed, stamping his feet,

while his pale-blue eyes momentarily blazed with intolerance and disbelief. Walter expected to run the school himself, enjoying from the governors the same trust and confidence that he placed in his staff. He had lost no time in introducing the necessary reforms, but he was under strong pressure to take extreme measures, for example to pay science teachers at a grossly inflated rate. At one stage shortly before Science had been time-tabled for the bottom form, Walter claimed that he had introduced Science to the Lower School, at which one of the governers called him a 'liar'. No wonder Walter was vexed.

His last governing body meeting transcended vexation. Walter had remained determined to relieve his successor of the double burden of being housemaster as well as Headmaster. Dr Arnold himself had been of the same mind. Walter's solution was simple. Rugby was fortunate in having a day-boys' house, which customarily creamed the local grammar school by virtue of bursaries from the same Lawrence Sheriff foundation. Walter proposed that the Headmaster should act as housemaster of Town House, the somewhat archaic conditions in School House being more than adequate for day-boys, and that a new School House should be built on a conveniently central site. This arrangement would improve the status of Town House, please the local parents and create another boarding house. He had always felt that the small number of large boarding houses at Rugby limited opportunities for promotion for housemasters. On the night before the meeting at which the proposal was to be discussed, an Old Rugbeian governor went to the Chairman and persuaded him to drop the idea. It was for Walter an ill-considered and crass rebuff. Moreover, and with the meeting breaking up, there were neither thanks nor a proposal to mark the end of an outstandingly great headmastership. The moment came and went not with a bang but a whimper. Walter was deeply hurt.

The Chairman wrote afterwards to Walter at Cambridge

with a covering note apologising for the lateness of the letter and saying:

> At the November meeting of the governing body, which you were attending for the last time in your official capacity, I should naturally have said a few valedictory words on behalf of us all at the conclusion of our business, but since a number of our body were not there and others had to leave before the end, it seemed hardly the moment to express the gratitude and appreciation, which each of us individually and the governing body as a whole feel towards our retiring headmaster. We all wish to acknowledge (what only your own modesty can prevent you from knowing for yourself) the great debt that Rugby owes to your headmastership. Our only complaint is that we could have wished it longer. The respect and affection felt for you by the boys of every age speak for themselves and many of the younger Old Rugbeians continue to regard you as their friend and counsellor. The masters have come to appreciate more every year that mixture of firmness and decision with sympathy and humanity, which are the qualities of a good headmaster. Many of them, I am sure, would in your case prefer to say a great headmaster.
>
> Your devotion to Rugby must have occupied most of your waking hours, but this did not prevent you from standing forth as a champion of the public schools during the most critical years in their history. Rugby has been proud to provide such a distinguished chairman of the HMC for more than one period of office and to know that he was regarded with trust and admiration by a host of headmasters. We thank you for your great and lasting services to Rugby.

This letter made handsome amends. But the wound never healed and Walter never forgot.

Respect and affection were the key words in all the tributes paid to him, and the essence of his personality is to be found in the sermon he delivered to leavers in Rugby Chapel at the end of his last term in December:

> The process of growing up is essentially the process of developing satisfactory personal relationships with other people.

139

How are we to judge whether our relations with other people are satisfactory? We can, if we like, apply the simple criterion of self-interest. If I have a strong, self-assertive, dominating personality, which puts me in a position to get what I want by imposing my will on others, that may seem to me a perfectly satisfactory state of affairs; and the fact that people with whom I have to deal are hardly likely to regard it in the same light will be, from my point of view, completely irrelevant. I shall inspire respect, perhaps even fear, and if that fear and respect are combined with a good deal of dislike, what does it matter?

Well, unfortunately, in the long run it matters enormously. Nothing, I am convinced, is more absolutely demonstrated by experience than the truth that if we live our lives on this principle we shall be profoundly unhappy. We shall have ignored and wasted one of the most basic needs of our nature, the need to be loved. We all recognise the need in the very young – we know that a baby that is starved of affection practically pines away – and we all know what is meant by a deprived child. What we have to realise is that this need remains with us all our lives, and if we conduct our relations with other people in such a way that it cannot be satisfied, we shall remain, whatever our material success and prosperity, permanently stunted and immature and unhappy people.

Walter practised what he preached. He liked being spoiled and his devoted secretary spoiled him outrageously. When she retired after he had left, he came back and made a short speech at her leaving party: 'When I appointed Edna she never came to realise that I knew she was running me. I was happy to let her do it. It was the best appointment I ever made.'

Gravitas dignitas auctoritas, but above all *humanitas*.

8

POLITICS

Donald Wright

WALTER HAMILTON SERVED for thirteen years on the Committee of the Headmasters' Conference, from 1953 to 1966, and for four of them as its Chairman. Then, a year later and no longer a headmaster, he was invited to join the Committee of the Schools' Governing Bodies' Association and served on it for seven more years, four of them also in the Chair. During these twenty years no one served longer, and no one earned more respect. He gave us security. That is why no portrait of Walter will suffice without reference to them. What follows seeks to portray, with broad brush strokes in a book such as this, his part in matters of major significance to member schools – and also to parents (and politicians) at large.

To the outside world, the consideration and co-ordination, in private, of policies amongst schools, no matter how prestigious their names may be, is scarcely going to elicit more than a few flickers of passing curiosity. Only when such policies are represented in public, especially if they are controversial, have they aroused attention. Yet headmasters invited to stand for election to the Committee of the HMC have seldom declined the offer. This is especially true of the national Committee which consists of headmasters elected to it by the Conference's regional divisions, and also of a small number (seldom more than four) who are co-opted by the Committee itself. Walter was co-opted soon after his arrival at Westminster and never served in any other capacity, being reinvited three times. He certainly enjoyed, more and more, being 'in the know', and the status amongst his colleagues which membership conferred; but he continued to serve primarily because his personality, clarity and quickness of mind, and above all his judgement, were such that his colleagues would not allow him to go. A headmaster of the next generation said in later years, 'We felt pygmies in his presence.'

In the late 1950s two fundamental issues in education, selection and privilege, entered politics with a new intensity. Both have remained to overlap and interact to this day. For the Independent Schools the next twenty years were of major even critical importance such as neither the Headmasters' Conference nor the Governing Bodies' Association had experienced before.

In 1955, when Walter had first become Chairman of the HMC, he and others invited Michael Stewart, Labour MP for Fulham, and in later years Secretary of State for Education and Foreign Secretary, to speak at its AGM. He chose as his title 'A Socialist View of Public School Education', and his influence was one which contributed a renewed thrust and focus for what was to come. Walter described the talk as the 'most interesting item on our agenda for a very long time' and afterwards allowed discussion of it – nearly all of it sympathetic to the analysis – to continue for over an hour.

When you say you do not want politics in education, you mean that you do not want any socialist ideas in education. Yet every educational system partly affects and is partly influenced by the political and economic structure of the society in which it exists. To suggest that a comprehensive school might help people to understand and live in the twentieth century is regarded as a dangerous socialist attempt to use the educational system for political ends . . .

Public school education is good: parents get value for money, but such education is distributed on a privilege-and-income basis. Do you want such a permanently identifiable group of schools rather better than those open to the rest of the nation?

Stewart then proposed the outline of a plan whereby a Labour government would first announce that at some date in the future fee-paying would either be abolished, or would apply to only 25 per cent of a school's entry, and prohibit the establishment of schools for profit. One could do that straight away, he said, adding that an Independent Schools Commission would decide the method and kind of recruitment to fill the 75 per cent of places; and that Regional Boards, with public school representation, would decide which pupils would be allocated. Each school would have the right to decline a pupil, having decided the level of its dullest boys. There would be little restriction on the schools otherwise.

The great gain to the nation would arise from entry having been 'democratised'. 'If you do not accept a change such as this, what will happen to you when society has reached the point when it will not tolerate the privilege element of fee-paying schools any longer?'

In the discussion which followed Robert Birley asked, 'Suppose a man obtains, in a way which Mr Stewart approves, the sum of £1,000, that is to say he really deserves it, and considers that he has three choices: to buy his wife a mink coat, to join and pay the future subscriptions of an expensive London club for himself, or to send his son to a public school. Is it right that the man should be allowed to do the first or the second but not the third?' Stewart replied that the question went to the heart of the matter. He admitted its illogicality but said that in a democratic society if one wants to make changes by democratic means, changes must always contain a certain element of illogical compromise, simply because that is the only way to get people to accept changes at all in such a society ... 'But my philosophic answer

143

to Dr Birley is this. A parent who buys his child a public school education feels that he is doing the best he can for his child, and is praiseworthy to that extent. He is giving him the opportunity for a larger income, a more influential position, and a more enjoyable life; but he is also buying him a position into a privileged class, and fundamentally I do not believe that is a good thing for a human being to have ... Virtuous though the parent's intentions are the nature of the society in which he lives means that he is not really doing for his child the best that could be done.' The issue which shadowed the debate could scarcely have been more vividly put.

Meanwhile there was no united Tory view about the public schools' future. Angus Maude MP voiced a not untypical opinion when he told headmasters in the following year that the schools should be left alone to provide parents with choice, that a measure of public assistance was harmless, and as to purchasable privilege and advantage 'the middle classes favoured improvements in the grammar and primary schools'. 'Arguments about privilege and advantage', he added, 'are rarely profitable: Independent Schools should continue so as to provide an element of competition for the Maintained Schools.' Meanwhile, 'if inflation continued and threatened the fee-paying schools, it would be no bad thing to reopen the list of Direct Grant Schools from time to time.'

There were 174 of these schools, of which 56 were in membership of the Headmasters' Conference. Each received a capitation grant direct from central government and in return was bound contractually to make at least 25 per cent of its places available without payment, the fees being paid by local government. For fee-paying pupils there were fee remissions related to parental income.

Walter, like many other headmasters, was very uneasy about the hesitancy and inactivity of the Conservatives. For him they undermined by default policies for widening the entry of public schools which not all, but a large number of

Scenes from the West Highlands.
Walter with Simon, Mull 1967 (top), *and*
with Robert and Charles, 1960, (left).
Ardbeg, holiday house on Mull (above).

With Caroline, Rugby, 1965.

Summerfields, Sports Day, 1969. Jane, Walter, Caroline, Catherine and Tim Burrows.

headmasters, for educational as well as political reasons, were looking for. Indeed he would have been content at that time to see all Independent Schools given an opportunity to go 'Direct Grant'.

Meanwhile the general unease with the eleven-plus, and with secondary modern schools, had sharpened social dissatisfaction with the grammar schools, and in 1958, at Scarborough, the Labour Party, by now anticipating a victory at the polls (which proved to be premature), had signalled its determination to reorganise maintained secondary education by requiring comprehensive secondary schools of, almost without exception, all local authorities.

At its AGM a month later the HMC staged its formal defence of the grammar schools. The form of the motion for debate was in four parts: opposition to a wholesale application of the untried comprehensive principle; the contention that, contrary to the national interest, such a step would lower academic standards; that 'the high quality of English secondary education depends on the traditions created by grammar schools, traditions which would be gravely endangered if the individuality of such schools were to be lost': and that the Conference deplored the ever-widening gap between State and Independent schools.

Desmond Lee proposed the first two parts of the motion, and Walter the third and fourth. Known as the heavenly twins, they had become, since Robert Birley's departure, the two outstanding leaders of the Conference. Walter spoke as follows:

> We cannot fail to fear for the individuality of the grammar schools. I do not think that a school has to be a famous foundation with a history centuries long to have a strong individuality, and I believe that that individuality has a considerable part to play in stimulating the achievements of its pupils ... Whether a boy of average ability makes the best use of his talents is immensely affected by the kind of atmosphere in

his school, and the sort which is desirable to encourage him takes a considerable time to create. Comprehensive schools may be found ultimately to be capable of creating it, but they certainly have not had enough time to create it at present, or to convince us that they are able to create it. It would be wanton to destroy it in any single school where this atmosphere exists.

I would go further: some sort of selection by ability is absolutely necessary for it helps achievement. A boy who has succeeded in getting to a grammar school has a feeling of achievement; and that something is expected of him ... I would go so far as to say that I believe that a perfectly just and impartial person, faced with the hideous choice of retaining the public schools or retaining the grammar schools, would reluctantly regard the disappearance of the public schools as the lesser evil.

A devil's advocate might suggest to us that the destruction of the grammar schools would operate to our advantage, because parents might send their children to independent schools to avoid the comprehensives. This is a spurious argument. If a gulf opened between the independents and all other schools, leaving the independents in isolation as sole purveyors of a particular type of education, I believe their position would become practically untenable and that the arguments about perpetrating class distinction and creating privilege would be enormously strengthened.

So it is not simply from motives of altruism that I hope that the Conference will affirm its support of the grammar schools by an overwhelming vote. It seems to me that it should do so from enlightened self-interest as well. The only fear I have in seconding the motion is that support from this conference for the grammar schools may be something in the nature of a kiss of death.

The motion was carried without dissent.

Six years later, in 1964. the newly elected Labour government set up the Public School Commission 'to advise on the best way of integrating the public schools with the State system of education; for the purpose of the Commission public schools are defined as "those independent schools now in membership of the HMC, the GBA, or Governing Bodies of the Girls' School Association".' A year later, Walter now

Chairman of the HMC for the third time – spoke frankly to
Rugby's parents on Speech Day:

We are accused of being a divisive factor in society, indeed of
being mainly responsible for class distinctions in this country. I
don't for a moment think that this is true; an educational system
may possibly reflect the social structure of a people, but it does
not create it, there are countries in which private education is
almost unknown which are yet no less conscious of class
distinction than ourselves. But though we are not the cause of
class distinctions, our record with regard to them is not
absolutely unblemished. We have sent out into the world many
men with strong and active social consciences, but we also have
our less desirable products who in the past have given
themselves, on the score of their old school tie, airs of superiority
which nothing in their character or attainments justified them in
assuming. I say in the past because I believe that this is
nowadays so far from happening that most public school boys
are almost apologetic about their place of education, and only
too anxious to make themselves indistinguishable from their
contemporaries at large. But resentment dies hard, and we
cannot honestly say that we have never done anything to
provoke it; it is not simply caused by the spectacle of too many
Etonians in the House of Commons.

In an age such as ours it *is* increasingly anomalous and even
unhealthy that the advantages which some independent schools
have to give should be confined to the well-to-do. Public schools
ought to be more widely accessible; there are many boys who for
various reasons have a need, and particularly a need for
boarding education, which we can supply and the maintained
schools in their particular case cannot, and for longer than I
have been a headmaster the Governing Bodies' Association and
the Headmasters' Conference have been trying to persuade
successive governments to provide the finance which would
make this possible. Of course it would be a pretty expensive
operation – I do not need to remind this audience that a Rugby
education is a commodity which cannot be had on the cheap and
that its cost is constantly rising. If a benefactor from heaven
were suddenly to shower upon us a gift of a million pounds (to
provide the full fees for 90 boys) without conditions, I do not

think that the school could spend it in a way more beneficial to itself and to the country, than in endowing boarding bursaries for such boys who need what Rugby can give, but who are at present excluded for lack of means. And if the Secretary of State's intention is that assisted places be made available in public schools on a substantial scale, after a considerable period of time amounting to something like half the intake of the school – I can say with confidence that he will find that in both Governing Bodies and in headmasters the greatest willingness, indeed eagerness, to co-operate with him.

However, I regard it as the duty of a public school to retain its independence. It is often urged by our critics that if more people in important positions sent their own children to maintained schools they would see to it that the standards of maintained schools rose. I believe on the contrary that if there were no alternative to the maintained system for anybody we should all be as helpless to remedy its shortcomings as are those of any other state monopoly, such as the railways or the Post Office. And of all monopolies an educational monopoly seems to me to be the most pernicious.

I believe that a development for the public schools such as I have outlined would be quite consistent with the retention of what is valuable in our character and tradition; it would be a development not by any means dissimilar from that which has made Oxford and Cambridge accessible to a wider public in the course of this century. It would involve no sudden and violent breach with the past, but for that very reason it is idle to suppose that it would satisfy the root-and-branch egalitarians, who on their own principles cannot be content with anything short of the complete incorporation of the public schools into the maintained system. And here we must note that their principles ultimately involve the complete prohibition of fee-paying schools; to stop short at taking over merely the most prominent would be not only logically indefensible but in the long run futile; it would lead to their replacement by what from any point of view would be profoundly undesirable, a mushroom growth of new fee-paying schools populated only by the wealthy. For in the last resort this is a question of personal freedom. What we should aim at is the extension of freedom of parental choice in education over as wide an area of the population as possible.

But democracies as well as dictators can be tyrants: may I commend to you two sentences from J.S. Mill *On Liberty* which touch on this point precisely. 'There is a limit to the legitimate interference of collective opinion with individual independence. And to find that limit and maintain it against encroachments is as indispensable to a good condition of human affairs as protection against political despotism.'

The Commission will be embarking on a quite impossible task if it is expected to combine the gradual development of a wholly desirable policy of increasing integration, in a way which safeguards existing standards and is financially practicable, with that of gratifying the immediate emotional satisfaction of those who cannot see in the public schools anything but the expression of social attitudes of which they disapprove, and which they are ingenuous enough to think would lose such reality as they possess outside their own minds with the suppression of a certain number of well-known and sinister institutions. I do not envy those who have to solve this dilemma.

In 1967 the first Report of the Public Schools Commission, about the future of the boarding schools, was published. The 'leaks' which had attended its deliberations, and also its visits to schools, had brought it into considerable disrepute. Its proposals were detailed, complicated, and instantly derided by the annual Labour Party Conference, and then turned down by government: they were too expensive and difficult to apply for serious consideration. The Commission's membership had failed to cohere, its terms of reference had been too political to be sufficiently precise, and there were few who mourned its failure. But what for many had first seemed a realistic opportunity for development was lost.

Meanwhile it had come to be realised that the future of the Direct Grant Schools was not going to be considered separately by the Commission. As Chairman of the HMC Walter had been at the centre of consultations which took place, albeit indirectly, between the Commission and the Conference in 1965. By then it had become unreasonable, owing to its demands, for the chairmanship to continue for a second year. But the Committee was unanimous in wishing to re-elect him, and to consider no one else, for a further year

– one which 'could be so critical to us all'. With what was a heavy heart Walter assented: he knew it was a difficult and unwise moment for the captain to be replaced. The headmasters of the Direct Grant Schools trusted him, having come to perceive that his support was genuine and whole-hearted, and that he understood the significance of these schools.

Addressing the AGM of HMC in October 1966 Walter had felt able to predict that the schools within the scope of the Commission had the good fortune to feel sure that they were being made the subject of careful study as educational institutions. He went on:

> I only wish the same could be said of the generality of direct grant and maintained grammar schools. No clear pattern emerges from a review of the present position of the direct grant schools. Their immediate prospects vary according to the complexion of the local authorities with which they are negotiating, but over all alike hangs the threat that if they do not accommodate themselves to the comprehensive system the only alternative for them is complete independence or extinction. The plain fact is that their continued existence in any form which would make their present status meaningful is irreconcilable with the policy of universal comprehension, and nothing it seems to me is to be gained by our refusal to face the unpalatable truth. Yet in their present form many of them are among the most successful institutions in the country, and the only result of driving these schools into being fully independent would be the withdrawal of the opportunities they offer from a class of highly gifted children of small means which has hitherto benefited from them. It is hard to see how this can conduce either to social justice or to the national interest. We can only hope that when, as must ultimately happen in many cases, these issues are directly referred to the Secretary of State, he will at last recognise the realities of the situation and redeem the implied pledge given last year that the nation cannot afford to lose any good schools.
>
> Perhaps I may be allowed to express my personal conviction that without selection in some form and at some point in the process of secondary education the pursuit of academic excellence

will be frankly impossible. We in this country have never been in danger of pursuing academic excellence to any fanatical extent; we tend somewhat to distrust intellectual brilliance, and we are right to recognise that other elements in education are of at least equal importance. But never before have we found ourselves in a situation in which schools of high academic standing, whether independent, direct grant or maintained, are regarded as socially undesirable because of that very excellence, and if in the obsessive but chimerical pursuit of a Utopia, from which the spirit of competition has been eliminated, we persist in a policy which results in their destruction, I believe that we shall have taken a very long step forward on the path of national decline. What kind of sense does it make to complain that the proportion of pupils at Oxford and Cambridge from maintained schools is not high enough, and at the same time dismantle a maintained grammar school with an unrivalled record of success in Oxbridge scholarship and entrance examinations? And when to this is added the fact that this educational revolution is being forced without adequate resources at a time of great financial stringency and without any serious research having been conducted into its probable effects, one can be excused for feeling that one is living in a looking-glass world.[1]

The merchant in the parable seeking goodly pearls presumably subjected the object of his search to a pretty searching inspection before he finally plumped for it. My fear is that we are in danger of selling all that we have and buying at a cost in quality which in a ruthless competitive world we simply cannot afford, a pearl which when we have purchased it may well turn out to be a sham. Absolute equality of opportunity is eminently desirable, it would take a bolder man than I to question that; the trouble about it is that it's not procurable either by reorganisation or by any other method. No power on earth can make all schools equally good, but it may be possible to come a great deal nearer to making them equally bad. For some that may represent an advance; there will always be people who hold that if what is desirable cannot be enjoyed by all it should be enjoyed by none. The principle of the equalisation of

---

[1]Walter used to quote that 'a nation declines through a softening of the head, long mistaken for a softening of the heart'.

misery is dear to the human heart, but profoundly inimical in my belief, to human progress.

Please do not conclude that I am attacking the comprehensive school *per se*. Far from it; I fully recognise the potential excellence of a comprehensive school of adequate numbers in buildings designed for its special purposes and in a suitable environment. What I am deprecating, is the inflexible attempt which is being made to force all schools into the same comprehensive mould, from which no significant deviation is to be permitted, regardless of the standing and quality of standing institutions; and instead of aiming at an extension of choice in education over as wide an area of the population as possible, to sweep away such traces of it as exist in the maintained system. In these circumstances the existence of an independent sector of education, the existence of schools free to operate outside the narrow limits prescribed by the established educational face, becomes of absolutely overwhelming importance; it is a vital element in the well-being not of a particular class or section of society but of the nation as a whole.

In December 1966 Walter left Rugby. His time as Chairman of the HMC also came to an end. Frank Fisher, who had served on the Committee with him for over ten years and did not lavish compliments, wrote in a letter to him, 'I don't know what we shall do without you. You have managed to weld everyone together in the past two years – the talkers, the cautious, the pushers, and the impulsive. We are now of one mind and more effective than we have ever been before.'

However, Walter's time was not yet done. For soon after becoming Master of Magdalene he became a member of the Governing Bodies' Association, representing St Dunstan's. He was immediately invited to serve on its Committee, and then in 1970 was elected Chairman. For the next four years the GBA became more active than ever before, perceiving that the time was both propitious and urgent. The return of the Conservatives to power had come as a reprieve for the Direct Grant schools, whose funding had been reduced by the

Labour government. With Margaret Thatcher Secretary of
State for Education and Science the future of the direct grant
was largely in her hands.

In January 1971 Sir Hubert Ashton was Vice-Chairman of
the GBA and Chairman of the Direct Grant Joint (with HMC)
Committee, which was a body representing such Schools'
Governors, Heads and Bursars. He thereupon went with a few
other members to the Department of Education and Science
with proposals for the replacement of the direct grant by a
national scheme for assisted places. Margaret Thatcher was
present with her officials and said she would need to consider
the proposals herself. Four months later she told Ashton she
could not afford to approve the scheme because she believed it
would lead to a flood of independent schools seeking the new
status. She was finding it difficult to obtain Treasury funding
for the direct grant list as it was, and urged upon Ashton all
possible restraint. It had become clear that she no longer felt
able to trust some of her own senior officials in the Department,
implying that they were in cahoots with the Treasury.

With hindsight 1971 was a critical year. In July the two
Chairmen of GBA and HMC invited Margaret Thatcher to
a private lunch to impress upon her the crucial importance
of the new proposals. However only during the final quarter
of an hour was direct grant even mentioned. She had nothing
new to say and with a flood of words dominated the
conversation, by talking non-stop on other matters. Six
months later Mrs Thatcher made a statement in the House
of Commons: she announced an increase in the amount of
the existing direct grant but in line only with past practice.
The new proposals were unacceptable. It was the end of the
road. When Labour returned to power three years later they
quickly phased out the grant, having felt no need even to
mention it as an issue in their election manifesto.

Walter had no first-hand experience of Direct Grant
schools. He gave strong backing of course to the Direct Grant

153

Joint Committee and could have done little more. A more imaginative and well-tried Secretary of State, with real feeling for the unique and national contribution made by these schools, might have achieved more. It was not as if the Tories were concerned to protect the entry lists of the comprehensive schools all that much.

However, bound as she found herself to be by the financial constraints of government, Margaret Thatcher turned on all the independent schools, challenging them to abandon hope of more central funding, not only for the direct grant but for boarding places in other schools too for children in need of them. 'You should learn to stand more on your own financial feet,' she said, strongly asserting that we should enlarge our share of the national entry, and 'demonstrate more confidence and independence. You keep talking about your wish to widen your entry, but what are you *doing* about it?' she asked.

This time the road led on to success. During the Public Schools Commission's deliberations the need for liaison and co-operation between GBA and HMC was greater than ever before, and when in 1964 the Commission had been set up a Joint Working Party was formed, consisting of six Governors and six Headmasters of whom Walter was one. A year after it had completed its work, another was formed in 1967 to make recommendations to improve the Independent Schools' public relations. Its principal recommendation in due course was that the schools should have their own information service, financed by themselves; that it should be regionally organized but with a national director, working from an office in London and supported by a proven public relations firm. The primary function of such a service would be to provide information about member schools for parents knowing little or nothing about such schools, or simply not enough. Meanwhile Margaret Thatcher's Under Secretary of State had attended a private session of HMC in 1971 to keep her in touch with developments.

At the next meeting of the GBA Committee Walter straight away proposed from the Chair that the recommendations of the Working Party be accepted. Already the new proposals for the Direct Grant Schools were to the front. Now the ones for the information service were also expedited. 'If we break through into different social strata', Walter said, 'that will be a great source of strength to all our schools. The parents don't know how to find out about us.' First there was a feasibility study, which was positive. Then the need to bring together all the Associations, including the Preparatory Schools and, belatedly, the Girls' Schools Association and their Governing Bodies. This task required patience and diplomacy, for the headmistresses – understandably – were defensive, and also frightened of where especially the more powerful boys schools might lead them. The costs of setting up and running the service would be substantial; the GBA must expect their governing colleagues of the schools to vote the money. A promotions committee was set up, whose chairman, Kirkpatrick Young, an enlightened chartered accountant, brought a flair which took aback many traditionalists. A budget was drawn up. Some of the bigger schools, thinking they had no need of assistance with entries, were shamed into support. A special meeting of the GBA was called to approve progress so far. It did so. By the summer of 1972 the girls' schools had become enthusiastic, and the preparatory schools were ahead of them; indeed they had been ahead of GBA and HMC all along. By now three important appointments had been, or were about to be, made and Walter was the moving spirit in seeing to all three of them: Kirkpatrick Young as chairman of the Promotions Committee, Joyce Cadbury as chairman of the Information Service's Joint Committee, and – most successfully of all – Donald Lindsay as its first Director. Each of these were supremely equipped to carry through the tasks that fell to them. Walter knew each one personally and freed them to make their own decisions.

In 1973 a second special meeting of the GBA was called. It gave unqualified approval to all its Committee's initiatives. By the end of the year ISIS was established and with a head office. When soon afterwards a general election was called the schools were well prepared for it. Information about them was sent to all MPs and peers. Roy Hattersley put Labour's case against the Independent Schools at length and St John Stevas (as he then was), Under-Secretary of State, was well briefed with a detailed and effective response. Hattersley was subdued. Labour's campaign faded, and so as a political issue has private education since that time.

Sadly the Direct Grant Schools had not been saved. But the GBA had galvanised itself, under Walter's leadership, so as to enlarge the number of parents who were to decide to send their sons and daughters to the independent schools, especially – and predictably – the day schools. Nearly twenty years later ISIS has fulfilled the hopes of its founders and demonstrated its value to the general public. For the rest of his life Walter however remained dismayed about the passing of the grammar schools, and almost equally pessimistic about the loss of Direct Grant Schools; the first owing to 'social engineering' or misplaced idealism on the Left, and the second, at least partly, to insufficient political vision and will on the Right.

In 1974 a successor as Chairman of the GBA was found, and Walter retired in that year. His record of endeavour should stand for itself in the light of subsequent developments. It was, and remains unsurpassed.

9

EDUCATION AND THE
SEARCH FOR TRUTH[1]

Walter Hamilton

THE SUBJECT WHICH I have been asked to treat is education
and the search for truth, a theme so vast that a far better-
qualified speaker might quail at the prospect. What kind of
education, you may ask, and what kind of truth, or, if it
comes to that, what kind of search? May I take the last
question first, and try to illustrate it by something quite
concrete, the situation which existed in Athens in the fifth
and fourth centuries BC?

The fifth century BC, like our own, was a time of great and
rapid intellectual change. Old certainties and old pieties were
being exposed to damaging criticism, while at the same time
success in life, in that small and intensely contentious society,
was coming to depend more and more upon an effective
mastery of the art of speech. Mother wit was no longer
enough; success in convincing a law court or an assembly
required an increasingly elaborate technique, and to supply
teaching in that technique was the chief function of the first
popular educators in history whom we call the Sophists. Old-
fashioned people regarded their teaching as immoral; it
enabled a man, in Aristophanes' phrase, to make the worse
appear the better cause, without regard for truth, and many
of the most celebrated sophists, like Gorgias and Protagoras,
were in fact sceptics. As Professor Guthrie puts it in his
history of Greek philosophy. 'If there is anything that may be

---

[1] A lecture given in Guildford Cathedral, 1970.

spoken of as a general sophistic view, it is this, that there is no "criterion". You and I cannot, by comparing and discussing our experiences, correct them and reach the knowledge of a reality more ultimate than either, for there is no such stable reality to be known. Similarly, in morals, no appeal to general standards or principles is possible, and the only rule can be to act as at any moment seems most expedient.'

Into this situation, which I think many of us would be willing to accept as a situation by no means wholly unlike our own, came a man called Socrates. Socrates may well have shared the scepticism of the Sophists so far as knowledge of the external world was concerned, and in moral matters he was so far from being an unquestioning upholder of conventional notions that his relentless puncturing of the complacency of his contemporaries led ultimately to his death. Nevertheless the gulf which divided him from the Sophists was profound, though he was often confused with them in the popular mind; it is one of the great ironies of history that his enemies were able to exploit the prejudice which existed against Sophists as a contributory factor in securing his condemnation.

To Socrates the material success to which sophistic education professed to hold the key was perfectly valueless. For him the only knowledge worth seeking was knowledge of how one ought to live; it is hardly going too far to say that he discovered the soul, which he declared that it is man's true business to make as perfect as possible. And he believed that such knowledge is attainable, though he was far from supposing that he had himself attained it; it is to be attained by honest and rational discussion between like-minded people, partners equally bent upon discovery of the truth.

But can such a search for moral principles of universal validity be pursued in isolation from the search for truth of a much more general kind? It soon became apparent that it could not. Plato, the devoted admirer of Socrates, who set himself to explore the implications of his master's teaching and in particular of his dictum that 'virtue is knowledge' found that his search involved him in the construction of an elaborate metaphysical theory, which in its turn required difficult and concentrated study of questions in logic and mathematics. For the pursuit of these studies he established the Academy, over whose door was inscribed the intimidating warning: 'Let no one enter who is ignorant of geometry.' This meant a good deal more than the warning which bars the way to contemporary universities: 'Let no one enter who has not a pass at ordinary level in mathematics or a scientific subject.'

In the next generation the search for truth took a somewhat different and to us more familiar form in the Lyceum of Aristotle. For Plato, however far he advanced into the abstractions of metaphysics, the motive of his search remained moral and political; his philosopher when he has attained the goal of truth is to descend again into the 'cave' to apply what he has learnt for the reformation of society. Aristotle on the other hand was a man of quite different temperament; what fired him was the disinterested pursuit of knowledge for its own sake; he wanted to understand rather than reform, and to him we owe the first systematic mapping out of the various fields of scientific and philosophical enquiry, ranging from ethics and politics to biology and physics, with a fully developed scheme of metaphysics and logic on which they are based. His colossal intellectual activity established him for centuries as the authority *par excellence* in all these fields of study, and we can discern in the Lyceum something very like a modern university, though it was a university in which all the chairs were held by one man. When they were not engaged in lectures and discussions the students of the Lyceum were occupied in research. They were put to the task of collecting historical and biological data for

Aristotle to systematise, and in this respect they were the counterpart of the research teams which frequently work for a modern professor.

I have dwelt upon this development at some length because it exemplifies at a very early stage in the history of thought and as it were in the clear light of dawn, two different aspects of the search for truth, the search for truth about man as a moral being, and the search for truth about the external world. There are, of course, other kinds of search for truth – there is for example the search for truth about God of which the Old Testament is the record – but you will forgive me, I hope, for selecting the topics with which I am most familiar.

I turn now to the second limb of my subject, education. How is this to be related to the search for truth?

One element in education has always been the transmission of the practical knowledge necessary for the continued existence of society, knowledge which has become immensely more complicated and specialised with the ever-increasing complexity of our ordinary life. Such practical knowledge ranges from the lowest level of literacy and numeracy, the three Rs, to the kind of expertise required, for example, by a computer-engineer or a surgeon; it includes everything that we can put under the heading of vocational education, and a good deal more besides; and training designed to enable men and women to make a career for themselves, and at the same time contribute usefully to the needs of society, has always been and remains today one of the most important concerns of education even at the highest level. We need, perhaps, in this connection to remind ourselves that the objects which originally inspired the foundation of universities were practical; what moved kings and bishops and great men to found and support them was the need for a supply of qualified men to conduct the business of Church and State, the need in fact for a professional class.

There is nothing dishonourable or mean in such a function
– and it will be a bad day for society if universities ever seek
to shed it – it was after all the function which Jowett made
the chief concern of Balliol at the height of its fame – but it
does not come much nearer to exhausting the content of
education than the training given by the Greek Sophists.

More fundamental and more relevant to my theme is the
task of education to preserve and transmit to successive
generations the culture of the past, using the term culture in
the broadest possible sense, to ensure that what has been
painfully won in the way of civilised values is not again
swallowed up by the barbarism which is always threatening
to engulf it, whether that barbarism is the barbarism of the
Goths or the barbarism of what has been called in our own
day scientific militarism. Education in this sense involves the
transmission of moral and religious as well as intellectual
values; its aim is to produce not well-qualified craftsmen or
technologists or professional administrators, but good and
cultured men, though I do not for a moment mean to imply
that the two aims are mutually exclusive. One of its marks is
that it values knowledge not for any practical ends that it can
be made to serve but as good in itself, as something which
enables a man to grow to his full stature.

How is all this related to the search for truth? Bear with
me, please, if I go back for a moment to Plato and Aristotle.
I have said, or at least implied, that the Academy and
Lyceum were the first universities; I might add that they
were the only universities which have ever been exclusively
devoted to the search for truth. In them education and the
search for truth were so closely linked as to be practically
identical. First, they were presided over by men of prodigious
creative genius; secondly, their membership was restricted to
a gifted few; thirdly, and this for my present purpose is the
most important, they were able to pursue the search for truth
in a spirit of perfectly free enquiry because the fields in which

they were educating their pupils were to all intents and purposes virgin fields, and they were unhampered by the obligation to transmit either the practical skills or the traditional culture which have since formed so large a part of the content of education. The discharge of these functions is clearly not the same thing as the search for truth; what may not be so obvious is that for long periods of history it has constituted a positive impediment to it.

If this seems at first hearing a startling paradox I would ask you to consider the implications of the fact that for centuries the culture which it was the task of education in the Western world to transmit was a culture based upon the twin pillars of Christianity and the Classics. It was therefore a culture within which in many fields no search for truth was possible, for the simple reason that you do not and cannot conduct a search for something which you are convinced that you already possess. And, of course, it was not only in matters of religion and morals that truth seemed for so long to be finally and unshakeably established. The authority of a verbally inspired Bible precluded enquiry in many other fields, notably of course in the field of science. History was contracted to a span of a few thousand years between the creation and the second coming; space was finite; species were immutable. Even where the authority of the Bible did not extend, the authority of the classical writers stepped in to fill the gap. The truth about geometry was to be found in Euclid, the truth about physics in Aristotle, the truth about medicine in Hippocrates and Galen. The great discoveries by individuals of genius which have transformed man's view of the world and of himself had to fight for recognition against a dominant educational orthodoxy. There is no time or need to multiply examples; I will simply remind you of the hostility with which the educated world of their day received the discoveries of Galileo and Darwin.

I hope that no one will make the mistake of supposing that

I am denigrating the Christian tradition in education. I am myself by nature and training deeply traditional, and no one in his senses would attempt to minimise the enormous benefits which education has received from the protection and support of the Church. It kept civilization alive through the Dark Ages, and until relatively recent times its activity in providing education for people of all classes has been in startling contrast to the neglect of the whole matter by the State. The point which I am making is simply this, that in any society in which a dogmatic world-view is firmly established – and I may say in passing that the record of contemporary Communism in this respect contrasts unfavourably with that of the medieval Church at its most intolerant – there is bound to be a tension, sometimes an almost unbearable tension, between the education whose function is to preserve and transmit that world-view and the search for truth whose function is to criticise it. Nor must it be forgotten that the Christian tradition has shown itself able to assimilate and to survive successfully vast modifications; it accommodated itself in the end to the heliocentric system, and, even more strikingly, at a much later date it has accommodated itself to discoveries which have pushed back the birth of the world into the unimaginable past and completely transformed our view of the origin and history of man.

I have skimmed in the most superficial way over these immense topics to give myself room for some reflections on the development of modern times. In this century for the first time since Aristotle the search for truth has again become one of the main preoccupations of universities, and if in what I now say I confine myself to universities – and to universities in this country, of which alone I am competent to speak – I think that you will agree that this implies no departure from my central theme.

I have tried to show how and why an educational tradition

whose function is to preserve and transmit an established world-view must inevitably present something of an impediment to the search for truth. It need not be a fatal impediment, but in the English universities by the end of the eighteenth century it had practically become so. However deeply one values Christian education it is impossible to deny that by that time the embrace in which the established Church in this country held Oxford and Cambridge was so suffocating as to be almost a hug of death. The great stream of the Christian tradition had become a mere trickle channelled through the sluggish veins of the Church of England, to which membership of the universities was strictly confined; non-residence and plurality were common among the senior members, as in the Church at large; such academic exercises as existed were of the most barren and arid nature; and the official teachers had almost entirely deserted the task of teaching. Let me give two illustrations from my own University of Cambridge. In 1764 Dr Richard Watson became Professor of Chemistry, having as he said himself, 'never read a syllable on the subject nor seen a single experiment in it'. Seven years later he exchanged his chair for the lucrative Regius Professorship of Divinity, though, to quote his own words again, 'he only knew as much divinity as could be expected from a man whose time had been fully occupied in other pursuits'. Finally in 1782 he became Bishop of Llandaff, and in 1787 retired to Westmorland, took to farming and died there twenty-nine years later, still Professor and still Bishop. My second illustration concerns the standard of achievement in a university in which even then the study of mathematics had pride of place. In 1788 Henry Gunning was 5th Wrangler; he tells us that at his examination 'the first and second problems were for the extraction of the square and cube roots, and, what was never before heard of, everyone was requested to attempt them as far as three places of decimals'. If you wanted enlightened and advanced teaching in the eighteenth century the only place in which to find it was a dissenting academy.

From this moribund state the old universities were redeemed by the gradual loosening of the shackles which bound them to the Church. This was a long process. Conservative opinion both in the universities and in Parliament fought a dogged rearguard action; it was only in 1871 that the last barriers in the path of dissenters and non-believers were removed. Since that time all universities and all university posts have been open to adherents of all religions or of none, and he would be a bold man who ventured to maintain that there is no connection between this fact and the enormous advances which the last hundred years have seen in the search for truth.

The advancement of knowledge in all fields is now generally recognised to be one of the principal functions of a university; it is what distinguishes it from other places of higher education. Have we then returned to the happy state of the Lyceum of Aristotle, in which all the students were engaged in the advancement of knowledge? Obviously we have not. A modern university, in spite of the enormous and, some may think, the exaggerated emphasis which it places on research, contains a large preponderance of undergraduates who have no taste or aptitude for any such thing, and who are there, in theory at any rate, for one of two educational reasons to which I referred earlier, and which must not however be thought of as mutually exclusive. They are there, or ought to be there, either for the wholly respectable purpose of obtaining a vocational training which will enable them to pursue a useful career as doctors, or lawyers, or engineers or whatever it may be. Or they are there for the much more nebulous, but equally respectable purpose, of broadening and maturing their minds by the disinterested study of subjects with no obvious practical application: pure mathematics or history or literature or philosophy and so on.

How can these by no means easily compatible ends be achieved within the single institution which we call a university? What is the cement which has so far held together a community which contains – and rightly prides itself on containing – people of every race and creed, every background and upbringing, every shade of moral and political conviction, a community, moreover, which owing to the sheer mass of knowledge to which research is always adding (knowledge, I make bold to add, by no means all of it of equal value) has become more and more a community of specialists, each pursuing the search for truth along a path which to most of his colleagues is probably unintelligible? The more one thinks of the strongly divisive factors which exist in any university, the more wonderful it seems that they have hitherto performed their hybrid functions so well.

Partly, of course, the universities, like society as a whole, have been held together by tradition. I do not mean simply the traditions attaching to any particular institution; these of course are powerful; I mean much more what may be called traditional attitudes. The final abolition of religious tests in 1871 did not result in a sudden dramatic change in the character of universities. It has taken quite a long time for them to become purely secular – though the newer ones, of course, have never been anything else – and it has not been till our day that a moral code which had survived the decline of the faith on which it was based seems finally to have lost its hold upon a considerable part of the academic population.

More specifically, however, the philosophy which has held the disparate elements in a university together and which has replaced the common faith of an earlier age has been a liberal optimistic belief in the supremacy of intellect, a belief that a man's mind is the most valuable thing about him, and that to be engaged on intellectual problems is the most valuable of all human activities, and is bound ultimately to lead, even if it is sometimes not clear how or when, to beneficial results.

There is much to be said for such a philosophy, prone though it is to estimate a man's worth too exclusively in terms of his mental ability; one of its most important effects has been to engender a large tolerance between people of even violently opposed views; any opinion is respectable in a university provided that it can be supported by intelligent argument. It has to be pointed out, however, that tolerance, desirable though it is, can never supply the place of conviction. The weakness of the current academic philosophy that I have been attempting to describe is that it is compatible with an almost complete scepticism, as great as that of the Greek Sophists. It is a philosophy of means rather than ends; it is in danger of valuing the search for truth for itself rather than for the truth which is its object, and if I had to find a motto for it, it would be this: 'to travel hopefully is a better thing than to arrive.'

It has, besides, practical consequences of an important kind. Because of its belief in the supremacy of the intellect, the academic mind tends to regard questions on which truth cannot be established with the rigour of a mathematical demonstration as open questions; there is always something to be said on both sides. It is a corollary of this attitude of conscientious open-mindedness that academics find it difficult to adopt a definite position on many serious moral issues, and exercise authority only with reluctance; this is because as a class – although of course there are countless individual exceptions – they do not find it easy to commit themselves unreservedly to the acceptance of any pro-positions of absolute validity, from which alone authority can be derived.

If my description of what I have called the academic philosophy of our day seems unduly harsh, it is because I want to depict it at its most vulnerable. I know quite well that it incorporates principles of inestimable value, principles which have moral and spiritual as well as intellectual

167

implications. I mean such things as the belief that the cultivation of the mind is a good thing in itself, the desire to set back by research what Housman called the 'frontier of darkness', the hatred of nonsense and intellectual humbug, and above all the conviction that disputed questions can and ought to be settled by rational discussion. Without these things anything beyond purely utilitarian education would be impossible; they are vital to the survival of civilization. But they will not avail the universities, and will not indeed survive themselves, unless the universities can somehow find their soul; they need to embark on the kind of search for truth which Socrates instituted, the search for unchanging principles by which to conduct one's life. Communities need such principles no less than individuals, but for universities, which, as I have said, embrace every shade of opinion and to which, owing to the enormous expansion of recent years, an increasing proportion of their members, both senior and junior, no longer bring an inheritance of what I have called traditional attitudes, such principles are now hardly easier to discover than they are for society as a whole.

It is so often supposed that relevance is to be found only in what is contemporary. Nothing is a surer sign of what I can only call the new barbarism than contempt for the past. I am myself quite convinced that exclusive concentration on what is contemporary is particularly unfavourable to the search for truth because it is so difficult to discuss contemporary issues without having one's judgement clouded by emotion and prejudice.

The philosophy of liberal optimism which has prevailed in universities and which in this country has not served them badly during the last hundred years rests on the assumption that human beings are fundamentally reasonable and that truth by its very nature is more attractive than falsehood. It is an assumption very like the assumption made by Socrates that virtue is knowledge, but unfortunately, like Socrates' assumption, it is very far from being universally true. Socrates believed that if a man knew what was right he would have no difficulty in acting in accordance with his knowledge; that was, no doubt, the case with Socrates, but for the generality of mankind St Paul was much nearer the mark when he said, 'to will is present with me, but how to perform that which is good I find not'. So it is with the search for truth; those rare beings for whom it has a supreme attraction above all other values do not easily comprehend that for most people the compelling power of truth is slight; one has only to consider what it is that sells the popular press to realise how slight it is. The search for truth requires self-discipline and precision of thought and a certain humility; for how many people do these austere virtues hold much attraction when they are placed in competition with the lures of excitement or publicity or power?

I believe that a main function of education is to protect civilised values against the barbarism that is always threatening to overwhelm them. In this country that threat is graver and closer now than at any time since the reform of the universities; all of them, though in very varying degrees, are threatened from within. They are not threatened by agitation of those who are genuinely concerned with the search for truth, genuinely concerned to discover moral principles on which a better society can be founded. The threat comes from those who believe that their ideals can be promoted by methods which violate the elementary principles without which no search for truth at all can be conducted, who deride the expression of views contrary to their own, and who think abuse and slogans a sufficient substitute for rational argument. May I quote to you a passage from an author unknown to me which I found recently in a commonplace-book? 'Ideals of any sort are dangerous visitants to vain and shallow minds. In the soil of a poor nature such minds bear ugly fruit in arrogance and insolent pretentiousness.' I have no hesitation whatever in saying that there should be no place in a university for such as these.

As I see it, then, the force of darkness against which the search for truth in our day has to contend is not, as in the past, the obscurantism of an established orthodoxy but a form of barbarism which regards truth as expendable in the struggle for power, the barbarism of the 'smear' and the slanted story, and on a larger scale of the propaganda lie. Against these, as was shown clearly enough by the failure of the German universities to withstand the monstrosities of National Socialism, the philosophy of liberal optimism is ineffective. How is it to be reinforced? I do not know. But to educators, whether in universities or outside them, I say that our only hope consists in returning to the rock on which our civilisation has been founded, and in reaffirming with conviction the eternal truth, from which man in his delusion of self-sufficiency is always trying to escape, that 'the fear of the Lord is the beginning of wisdom'.

10

MAGDALENE

Master 1967–1978

From the *College Magazine and Record*, October 1988

WALTER HAMILTON'S WHOLE life was dominated by a symbiotic movement back and forth between the world of schools and the university. If the former proved in the final analysis to have been his true métier, it was at Cambridge that his most creative and influential work was done. His feelings about academia were, however, decidedly ambivalent, and he was never entirely satisfied by his performance within it. Teaching was his first love, and where he really excelled.

There were no doubt several reasons why his return to Cambridge in 1967 was to bring him less satisfaction than might have been expected. It coincided with a period of unprecedented student unrest, the animus and naïvety of which depressed even the youngest don. The Magdalene version of it was not as virulent as elsewhere, but our problems were compounded by the almost inevitable 'sixties' drugs scandal. More generally, the world of scholarship had moved on, with increasingly seismic shifts of approach even in Classics. Despite some erudite early work on Plutarch, Walter never had much sympathy with contemporary research. He even found the astringency of modern academic reviewing rather distasteful.

Then, as far as the Mastership of Magdalene is concerned, the ancient system under which the Fellows do not choose their own head means that any incoming Master is particularly on his mettle, although he knew we welcomed a scholarly educationalist at the Lodge. At his first Governing Body meeting he assured the Fellows that he fully understood the difference between a headmaster and a Master. This observation went down well, but he found it difficult in practice to make the necessary transition. He much disliked Governing Body meetings. Those who did not know him well may also be surprised to learn how diffident he could be. Nor did he feel it was easy to succeed Harry Willink, after whose ebullient management and conversation, his own quieter, unpretentious style was a distinct contrast. In fact, it was in many ways a relief. Some sort of administrative pause was probably desirable after a hectic period of improvements in all directions. Walter's Mastership was certainly not without its achievements, however, such as the steady development of academic facilities, and consolidation on the financial front. It is largely owing to him that Denis Murphy succeeded Jock Burnet on his retirement as Bursar. Also, it was on his initiative that Andrew Wallace-Hadrill, Tom Howarth and James Hunt were brought to the College, all of whom made, in their various ways, significant contributions. Walter was responsible, too, for one major new departure: limited-tenure teaching posts. But in general he regarded it as part of his brief to keep things pretty much as they were, and especially not to capitulate rashly to merely fashionable demands for change. This undoubtedly served the College – and indeed the University – well during the student troubles, to which he brought a reassuringly strong hand, the envy of less fortunate institutions. There was not much in the way of building to be done. The new Master's Lodge was already on the drawing-board and he urged us to go ahead. Buckingham Court was completed during his tenure, and not least because of his successful approach to Humphrey Cripps for the necessary funds; but the basic planning in this case also was done before he took office. The lack of movement in admissions policy (of which he had charge for some years) was rather more surprising. Overall, then, there was a comparative lull in major projects and policy initiatives. Perhaps as a result personal issues came to seem more important than they would otherwise have done. He did not always handle them well; but it was not he who created them.

By nature, Walter thought of himself as being – like Dr Johnson – a lazy man. He enjoyed simple pleasures, such as a glass of whisky with a friend, or a stint of domestic wallpapering or 'destructive' gardening. He preferred small-scale intellectual challenges, from the daily crossword to intermittent wrestling with the obscurer parts of Plato. He loved quiet family holidays in Mull with Jane and their four children. However he was well aware that he must not be forever idling by still waters, and he could smite living fountains from the rocks to great effect. With the things that really mattered to him – putting Plato (and more recently Ammianus) into an accessible form for modern readers, preaching sermons in Chapel, serving as chairman of the local Examinations Syndicate, governing schools (including Shrewsbury, Eton and St Dunstan's), or making the Benson Diary available to the literary world – his capacity for taking pains was formidable. His stylish and authoritative translation of *The Symposium* for Penguin Classics was a stunning success; it has been reprinted 28 times and sold well over half a million copies. (It still sells 4,000 copies a year.) For the Local Examinations Syndicate he travelled the globe, a task which gave him something of a proconsular role on behalf of the University at large. He was a fine preacher: incisive, clear, humane, memorable. His presiding address at the funeral of I. A. Richards, a difficult occasion, was unerringly appropriate: dignified, kindly, eloquent, warm-hearted. As an interviewer he was anxious to help shy candidates do their best. And anyone with a problem would get a patient hearing and some good advice.

His physical presence was powerful, even austere in public at times. The famous melancholy Eeyore-like voice (so temptingly easy to imitate), the quizzically sardonic phrases, the over-prolonged rattling staccato laugh (never more disconcertingly infectious than when amused at his own jokes), the sheer bulk of him shifting with a sudden defiant stare over half-moon spectacles, the tactical mumbling into his beloved pipe: here was a figure begging to be used in a novel. Derek Hill's official portrait curiously diminishes him both in body and spirit. The man we knew was in every way larger than this. Nor was he always quite so unequivocally benign, and to run foul of him, or bump up against one of his more troubled moods, could be distinctly uncomfortable.

At his best he was notably good-humoured, and he often used to laugh at himself. He rather enjoyed being a complex person, part Jowett, part Johnson, part Jeeves, part Jeremiah, except perhaps when the tensions and pessimism became too real. Although he sometimes wore his heart on his sleeve, he was fundamentally a reserved man, truly at ease only with his family, his dogs, or a few close friends who understood the world of schoolmastering. To those in his inner circle he was a rewarding, genial and lovable companion. Many boys and quite a number of undergraduates penetrated his defences; they enjoyed themselves hugely. He was called to the College's highest office at a difficult time, and discharged it faithfully and with costly devotion, but his unease with modern university life meant that he was not wholly suited to it; and indeed he was himself too modest a man to feel that his Mastership would be assessed entirely eulogistically. But he was without a doubt a profoundly good man, a sound scholar, a revered teacher, a rich character, widely admired well beyond Cambridge, fondly regarded by many, and there is much regret at his passing.

Ronald Hyam

Publications

'The myth in Plutarch's *De Facie* (940F–945D)' and 'The myth in Plutarch's *De Genio* (589F–592E)', *Classical Quarterly*, XXVIII (1934), pp. 24–30, 175–82.

The Symposium by Plato: a new translation with an introduction (Penguin Classics, 1951, repr. 28 times).

Plato's Gorgias: translation with an introduction (Penguin Classics. 1960, repr. 13 times).

Plato's Phaedrus & Letters VII & VIII: translation with introductions (Penguin Classics, 1973, repr. 6 times).

Ammianus Marcellinus, The Later Roman Empire (AD 354 – 378); selected and translated by Walter Hamilton, with an introduction and notes by Andrew Wallace-Hadrill (Penguin Classics, 1986).

From Denis Murphy

I first met Walter when he served on the University's Council of the Senate during the early 1970s when Cambridge, in common with most universities, was being subjected to some very unpleasant behaviour by politically motivated under-graduates, some of whom did not stop short of criminal assault in their attack on 'the Establishment'. It is fair to say that the University was unprepared for that crisis; in any event the trumpet gave forth an uncertain sound. Not so with Walter. As one member of the Council (who differed from him) said: 'He represents the Establishment view: but he represents it intelligently.'

I was not present in the College during the 1970s but it is clear that Magdalene was not seriously affected by 'student troubles'. In large part, this relatively trouble-free zone was Walter's main achievement here. He once said to me that his Mastership was to be weighed more by what he had *not* done than by anything else. As every Bursar knows, the hardest thing is to say 'No', particularly to those one likes. Walter not only did this, in defence of vital College interests, but in the process he disarmed opposition with wit.

I was Bursar for only two years of his Mastership but the record shows that he presided over a major improvement in the College's finance and buildings. Furthermore he greatly raised Magdalene's standing in the University through his involvement on the Council of the Senate and its many Committees. If one must paint the picture 'warts and all', it must also be said that his very virtues (and especially his fierce loyalty to friends) got him into trouble at times in the College towards the end of his tenure. That is of no significance, however, when measured against the great contribution he made during the particularly difficult period for the College and the University.

Michael Dias adds:

It was during this period that Walter served his four years on the Council of the Senate, the University's top institution. When the biannual elections to the Council from the lower ranks were due, he urged me to stand for election since he felt that 'right-wing' support was needed there. I was elected in due course and we all had a difficult time. After a disastrous sit-in the then Vice-Chancellor decided to allow representatives of the protesters to come and address the Council. Four of us walked out of the Senate: Walter, Dr Clive Parry, Mr Geoffrey Switzer and myself. We met in Walter's room and presented the Vice-Chancellor with an ultimatum of our own to the effect that we would not return unless certain demands were met, including the setting up of a public inquiry into the disturbance under an outside Chairman. The upshot was the famous hearing under Lord Devlin, resulting in the Devlin Report, which introduced some major changes.

Above: *Royal visit to Westminster, 1950. Walter with Queen Elizabeth and, behind, John Carleton with King George VI.* Below: *Rugby 1960.*

With his portrait, which had just been painted for Magdalene by Derek Hill, 1975.

From Brian Deakin

My recollections of Walter include his quiet and notably skilful conduct of Governing Body meetings. He much alleviated the burden of the more tedious items of business on the agenda, which he dispatched with efficiency, dry wit and merciful speed.

I was greatly impressed by the large extent of his personal engagement in College business. For six years he conducted all the onerous work of admissions himself. He was of course well placed by his earlier career and experience to know well the school territory from which we drew most of our applicants, but he was always anxious to extend that territory and in fact did so in my subject with encouraging results in terms of some entrants of good quality and subsequent tripos performance. At meetings of the Admissions Committee he would require each Director of Studies to speak to his subject list. There remained marginal candidates in various subjects. Walter would then conduct a scrupulous and detailed appraisal of each of these. He demanded the file of each such candidate and read out and appraised as he went along the evidence from it – the Headmaster's report, examination results, interview notes. Comparisons were made across subject boundaries and were weighed. He did not 'read between the lines' of reports in any speculative sense, but his knowledge of headmasters and housemasters enabled him to interpret reports and to balance evidence in a way which was far beyond anything the rest of us could do. There was no hasty dispatch of business on these occasions. The meeting continued throughout the day, and often beyond.

The undergraduate 'troubles' of the late 1960s and early 1970s did not greatly influence the always good relations between Fellows and their pupils in College which Walter did so much to preserve and improve. Only one Magdalene undergraduate, a sociologist, out of more than a hundred present, was found at a 'sit-in' at the Senate House. In College Walter set up a Joint Committee of Fellows and undergraduates to discuss some aspects of College business and the real and imagined undergraduate problems of various kinds. This policy was successful in doing that and in maintaining and improving relations in College. When the Senior Tutor told Walter that a 'march' of undergraduates was approaching Magdalene on their way to demonstrate at the Shire Hall and might cause trouble along the route which included Magdalene Street, he replied: 'We shall be here!'

That there was very little of the 'we – they' type of feeling in College during the years of unrest among students generally can be attributed largely to his witty, human and friendly manner coupled with his imposing presence and the prompt deployment of his very considerable diplomatic skills.

From Robert Latham

I got to know Walter when I was Pepys Librarian from 1972 to 1982. Under the terms of Pepys's will the Library was to be 'under the sole power and custody of the Master'. In practice Masters remitted day-to-day management to a Librarian while retaining, with the Governing Body, responsibility for policy. During my tenure of office the matters of policy at issue mostly concerned the publication of a new edition of the Diary, and preparation for the construction and publication of a detailed and elaborate (and expensive) catalogue of the contents of the Library in nine volumes. Walter, who had had publishing experience as a director of Hodder & Stoughton, concerned himself with the business side of both projects, in co-operation with Jock Burnet, the Bursar. He was particularly active in connection with the catalogue, about which many decisions had still to be made when he assumed office. The Library benefited greatly from his wise guidance.

From Andrew Wallace-Hadrill

For a Rugbeian to come, ten years on, to find Walter ensconced in the Master's Lodge at Magdalene was at once to find a solidly familiar figure and a subtle transformation. Walter had made a grand and impressive persona of the headship of Rugby; as Master of Magdalene he was a grand figure too, but in a different way. At Rugby he was respected as a man of learning, who brought from Cambridge and the great world outside the school standards of academic excellence to which one looked up with reverence. It was like that too when he taught: others were professional schoolteachers who knew their job well; but he was an apparition descended from the skies, who had once touched the mantle of Housman and Gow, and could point back to the gods of classical philology, Bentley and Porson.

However, Walter's return to Cambridge had changed his relationship to the world of scholarship, a world in which for him the preoccupation with research had come to replace scholarship and learning, and the achievement of publication more significant than distinguished teaching. 'Research' summed up everything Walter regretted about the changes of academic life since he had left Cambridge.

As a figurehead, in particular for the undergraduates, he retained all of his old stature. He was above all in his element presiding over a College Feast. His speeches, whether to a hall full of undergraduates, ever on the brink of rowdiness, or to a solemn assembly of dignitaries at the Feast of Mary Magdalene, were a delight. Nobody I have known had his talent for combining complete dignity of presence with a sense of the absurd. His aphorisms remain in folk memory, but his secret lay in delivery and timing. There was always a delicate counterpoint between the lugubrious tone that led his listeners to expect pronouncements of great solemnity, and the sense of the absurd that undermined it.

As a chairman Walter was strong, as a politician adept. He sometimes found it irksome that academics not only had opinions of their own, but were prepared to insist on them with tedious tenacity. But he knew how to steer a meeting past such obstacles, with authority and despatch. If he sensed opposition, he could quell it in advance by intoning 'Well?' and traversing the table with a penetrating glare.

In many ways Walter gave the College just what, in troubled times of change, it wanted. He ruled over it with a sort of benevolent paternalism which, far from moving it into the student era created by Vietnam, Paris and the Garden House protest, harked back to a bygone age. In a deeply conservative college, he provided stability and a firm faith in traditional values.

From Christopher Greenwood

I went up to Magdalene in 1973. It was Walter's sense of style which first impressed me. Undergraduates tend to be influenced more by the personality of a Master than by the substance of his policies for the College. In a Cambridge which was becoming more uniform – at least in matters of style – and where dons were less evidently eccentric, Walter stood out as a distinctive figure. To the student activists of the late 1960s that may have been chiefly because of his conservatism, but to my less radical 'generation' it was the wit and the frequently self-deprecating humour with which he expressed that conservative philosophy which made him exceptional.

Walter's manner frequently deceived those who did not really know him. His somewhat melancholy voice – he would have been brilliant reading the part of Eeyore in a radio production of *Winnie the Pooh* – often made it difficult to realise he was pulling your leg. Meeting him at Cambridge station one winter evening I told him – perhaps rather pompously – that I was going to London for a meeting at one of the Inns of Court. 'Oh,' he replied, 'I'm going to London for a pound.' I was half-way to London before I realised he was taking advantage of a new pensioners' travel concession and that my own serious sense of purpose had been quietly deflated.

I joined the Fellowship at Magdalene the term after Walter retired. My chief memories of him come from my undergraduate days when I saw him as an imposing man, ruling over the College with great success at a difficult period in its history, yet doing so with great wit and human warmth. If in some respects he belonged to the Cambridge of an earlier age, he was undoubtedly the right Master for his time.

From Tim Kirkup

Those first hours in Cambridge are not easy ones. You collect a key, hang around notice-boards, queue punctually and quietly for dinner in Hall. You hunt out your personal tutor, your Director of Studies, your supervisors. You try out a few clumsy lines on strangers. You are addressed by the Senior Tutor, the Captain of Boats, the JCR President. The whole thing reminds you of starting school. You think about running away.

Enter Walter Hamilton, Master of the College. Having been intimidated by the Domestic Superintendent, you prepare for the worst. Instead you meet someone from the world you know, quietly spoken, benign, reassuring. Instantly, he engages with his undergraduate audience. A little unforced laughter takes to the air and you begin to feel a bit less bogus. This place might not be so bad after all.

Walter was popular with undergraduates, as two spontaneous cheerings at Second- and Third-year dinners indicated. He was infinitely more interested in undergraduates than most Fellows were, and I suspect he enjoyed their company more than he did that of the Fellows. Behind the imposing frame lay a shy man but an expert schoolmaster. He knew the right sort of questions to ask, could take a restrained delight in undergraduate enthusiasms, and, in moderation, had a ready and wise sympathy for their weaknesses. If all else failed, he could launch into one of his narratives, finishing with a flourish, striking the table hard, heaving back and forth on his chair, rasping with hilarity. He charmed his company – he knew it and he loved to do so. 'The trouble with me', he would moan, borrowing from the Master of Trinity, 'is that I haven't got any big talk.' It wasn't true, of course, but he had that knack of putting people at their ease.

It was sad then that he remained so much of a figurehead to so many undergraduates, known more in his caricature than in the flesh. The role of Master thrust remoteness upon him: there were simply too few *ready-made* opportunities for informal contact. There was an enjoyable risotto lunch in the first term; there was, indeed, an open invitation to all to look in on him after Dinner of a Sunday evening ('a little weak refreshment and weak conversation'). But undergraduates don't find it very easy to make the first move, and you need a more than average nerve to stroll up to the Lodge door to find out what sort of chap exists behind it. Walter should have encouraged more callers, engineered more opportunities. But he knew his clientele didn't live across the passage in the boarding house, and he was reticent about intruding.

I brushed up against Walter pretty early on. There was an absurd little ceremony to admit scholars over coffee with the Fellows. I suppose we must have chatted, for it came back later that I had been rude to him 'in a very nice way', and that he'd rather enjoyed it. And thus the teasing began. The first time the choir sang the Lord's prayer at evensong, I was chastised for training them to sing 'temp-ta-si-on'. Never again. Nor was I allowed to have the modern tune 'Abbots

Leigh' to accompany the hymn 'Glorious Things of Thee are spoken'. 'People have heard of Haydn,' he droned, 'which is more than can be said of C. V. Taylor.' Occasionally, I would slip in something to provoke him. 'Play that at my funeral ('God moves in a mysterious way') and I'll bang on the roof.' He hated the harpsichord, the spinet and the virginals, and he damned all their repertoire as 'tweedly-wheedly music'. I expect he hated organ recitals too, but he most dutifully attended mine.

Being a hospitable place, Magdalene bred in one the desire to reciprocate. Jock Burnet urged on my breezy instincts and persuaded me that great ones are not necessarily unflattered by student invitations. 'Ask Michael Ramsey to tea,' he would preposterously suggest. So I did. 'Have Walter and Jane round for a meal.' My elegant rooms commanded a superb view of the Cam but I had access to no more than two gas-rings. College regulations permitted the boiling of eggs and the making of porridge. Never one to press for clarification of rules, I smuggled in a Baby Belling and set to work in a cupboard. I served casseroles and crumbles washed down with Moselle, but at least the veg. was never overcooked.

Jock was right, of course: the Hamiltons were delighted, appreciative guests. After his retirement from Magdalene, Walter and Jane came to meet four of us in London to celebrate over a more sophisticated gigot of lamb. On the seventeenth floor of a Barbican luxury apartment block, Walter's sense of treat was unbounded, even childlike. 'An egg boiled very soft is not unwholesome,' he would simper, pretending to be Emma Woodhouse's father while he tucked into a large plate. 'Suppose we all have a little gruel.'

At formal guest-nights in each other's company we shared some hilarity at the antic fawnings of those who were awed by him. 'Nothing but a great heap of meat,' he whispered about a headmaster who dined opposite us on one occasion.

Walter was touched to be asked to such events by a young friend and was not the least bit interested in sitting next to the second most distinguished person present. 'Come and talk about Johnson, would you?' I asked him, in my second year of teaching at Christ's Hospital. I mustered a decent audience and introduced him. He looked suddenly older, even a bit gaga; his eyes moved uncertainly between his script and me, seated on the extreme right. The delivery was slow and monotone. I shifted uneasily and looked down at my knees, willing him to make contact with other people in the room. Inwardly I appealed to the boys to sit it out and not be disrespectful. And then there was loud laughter, and I realised that the old fox had been stringing us along all the time.

In the mid-1970s, Magdalene seemed to be stuffed with those who knew about schools. I was a little wary of this. Though I had long wanted to teach, I maintained an obstinately independent line in the face of all the public school reps. that I found around me. Walter would have been happy – indeed, he would have been delighted – to help fix up a schoolmastering post for me. But, possibly because our educational backgrounds were quite similar, he had a respect for my stubbornness and allowed me to go about the business in my own way. He was courteous like that, but it didn't stop him being amused at my expense.

'How are all those terrible Wykehamists treating you?' he wrote when I was temporarily working at Winchester. 'Jane and I think you had better come to Mull to flush them out of your system.' I went, and paid dearly for being temporarily attached to a quite innocuous naval cap. Early-morning tea was served with a hearty salute from Ben Jonson: 'Thou look'st like Anti-Christ in that lewd hat.' (Later, it was my beard that gave offence: what did I need to hide behind all that fuzz?) When I embarked on my first job, my soft liberal tendencies had been astutely noted.

Walter advised on the only sure way to schoolmastering success: 'Get a good mark-book, and establish a reign of terror.'

It didn't do to take oneself too seriously with Walter, but you knew that you had to be an intimate in the first place in order to be teased at all. Nevertheless, Walter was himself often in need of cheering up. 'Oh, I don't know,' he would groan as he drew back the door, 'I'm feeling rather low, actually.' He would pour out a little of 'the whisk', but he affected to do so grudgingly since, he claimed, I would need something to fall back on after I reached forty. Sometimes, he would unpack a few of his woes; at other times, he would let me rattle on while he brooded miserably behind grey smoke. The next morning I might receive a rather touching note: 'A visit from you was just what I needed. I feel much better today. Thank you.'

Walter was suspicious of the Cambridge English tripos and felt sorry for my having to grapple with its intricacies at all ('It's so hellishly subjective'). He offered to teach me Greek (now why didn't I take him up on that?) and he would lend me some of his Loeb texts of Virgil. He hoped that I might introduce him to some new authors. But he found much of twentieth-century literature, particularly poetry, perplexing, and he was splendidly intolerant of what he judged to be poor prose style. He fell back on his old enthusiasms, and he loved to share some of these with me. I had never read Housman, whom he had known. At his insistence, I read more Conrad. I re-read Jane Austen (we both delighted in Mrs Norris: 'I must keep a spare room for a friend'). Above all, I met Dr Johnson.

Walter gave me my copy of Boswell's *Life of Johnson* during my second year at Magdalene. It will be readily understood why the book is fondly treasured. On the flyleaf, in the right-hand corner, there is written:

W. Hamilton
Trin. Coll. Camb

Walter won it as a prize in 1929.

Underneath, in the same elegant hand, in the same blue-black ink:

Tim Kirkup
from W.H.
May 17, 1976

In 1978 Walter announced his retirement. Responding to Michael Ramsey at the farewell dinner, Walter said:

'The last twelve years have been times of great and almost unprecedently rapid change in universities and colleges. It is a satisfaction to me that Magdalene has changed more slowly than most and I only hope for the better. It has refrained from climbing on to some of the fashionable bandwagons, which roll with increasing momentum towards the abyss like Gadarene swine. But I cannot claim any particular credit for this. I only claim masterly inactivity – I use the word masterly of course in the Pickwickian sense.

'In spite of my past flirtations with the academic life at Trinity I am not really by temperament or talent an academic. I am glad not to have spent my whole life at Cambridge. But to have spent the last twelve years at Magdalene has been an almost unbelievable stroke of good fortune in what has been a very lucky life.'

11

THE GIFT OF WORDS

Andrew Wallace-Hadrill

I T WAS IN working together over the text of Ammianus that Walter and I had our happiest moments together, and got to know each other most closely. When he retired from Magdalene, he was worried about what to do with himself next. Tom Howarth perceptively urged him to turn his hand again to translation: 'What you need is some mental knitting.' Tom was right, for translation is a task that can be picked up in odd moments of freedom, and does not require sustained concentration. Walter wrote to Betty Radice, and was rather dismayed to hear back from her that the only outstanding candidates for Penguin translation were the elder Pliny and Ammianus Marcellinus. Both authors were just about as far from his beloved Plato as they could be. But he allowed himself to be persuaded to give Ammianus a go; at least Ammianus' hero was the philosopher-emperor Julian, and he was the late Roman historian who most won Gibbon's admiration.

In the business of translating, Walter was truly in his element. Translation is not, in modern academic terms, 'research' (and were it so, Walter would not have loved it). It does, however, require scholarship: a deep knowledge of language, the rare ability to distinguish sense from nonsense, and a way with words. Walter had all these, and the way with words in a supreme degree. Whether it was in his sermons, or his after-dinner speeches which were one of the most treasured features of his Mastership of Magdalene, or in anything he wrote, from a formal memorandum to a personal note, his sense of style was unfaltering, and made all others look clumsy beside him. His classical training gave everything he wrote balance and polish; his philosophical training and acute mind gave it lucidity. He had to an exceptional degree an ear for the music of language, for its rhythms and falls; hence a love for the cadences of Johnsonian prose, and a dislike for the harsh baldness of twentieth-century English. But above all he had a gift for finding the right word. He shuddered at clumsy and inept words, and trendy cant of any sort; and would seize with glee upon the *right* word, repeating it to himself and savouring it: 'I do like so-and-so,' he would gloat, as he went over a passage, and hit upon a favourite word.

This is not to say that all was plain sailing with Ammianus. On the contrary, he detested his style, which is verbose, rhetorically overblown, and at its worst degenerates from rant into nonsense. Walter hated rant and nonsense, and was often in agonies as to how to represent his author's meaning and style without offending too grossly against his own stylistic sense. For that reason, his Ammianus does not reach the level of his *Symposium*, where translator was deeply in sympathy with author, and lucidity of thought and beauty of expression go hand-in-hand. Even so, it is a marvellous piece of work. Walter could bring to bear on this often turgid, but sometimes vivid, author his gift for undercutting a parade of pomp with a sense of the absurd.

He delighted, for instance, in Gibbon's characterisation of the author's style in the words, 'the coarse and undistinguishing pencil of Ammianus'. After the rolling epithet 'undistinguishing', the word 'pencil' falls with a glorious disdain. Walter would play this game again and again, rescuing his author from banality and pomposity by a delightful turn of phrase. Take the opening page of his translation. The first sentence is a virtually impossible one to handle, heavy with portentous metaphor. But Walter redeems it by word-choice: 'but before the trumpets had ceased to bray or the troops taken up their winter quarters cruel fortune let loose upon the state the squalls of another storm.' For me, the words which rescue the sentiment from collapsing under its own weight are 'bray' and 'squalls': they inject life and irony back into it. And they should of course be read aloud, like all Walter's prose, and spoken as he would have spoken them, lingering on the favoured words with rich and resonant vowel-sounds.

Look on down the page, and it bristles, as does every page in the volume, with unmistakably Walterish turns. Gallus was causing 'universal mischief' – the translator's understatement in choosing 'mischief' redeems the author's exaggeration in 'universal'. Fuelling the mischief are 'adroit secret dealers in backstairs gossip': Ammianus is too verbose to let a good translator get away with simply 'gossip-mongers', and Walter saves the periphrasis by the use of 'adroit', which so well describes his own verbal skill. Notice in general what he has not done, unlike so many a Penguin translator. He has not cut his author down to size, by putting his heavy rhetoric on a twentieth-century diet, draining away the colour, and leaving bland and pat contemporary journalese that slips past without noticing. Nor on the other hand does he ever slip into the ungainly translationese which so mars Rolfe Loeb's *Ammianus*, following the sense of the author's Latin without ever quite converting it into acceptable English. Walter's translation preserves the sense of strangeness of an author from a different thought-world, without once committing to print an expression that is less than English.

They were happy days together. I was supposed to do the history while he did the translation. But in fact I found myself for hours upon end arguing over turns of phrase. Often he needed encouragement, and sometimes he showed signs of despairing of the whole enterprise. He was far from satisfied.

But in the end there was a sense of triumph. He had tangled with a tough challenge, a long and recalcitrant text. He had wondered if he would ever live to see it published. But he did, and had to admit for all his apprehensions that it was a success. I can think of no better epitaph to the verbal skill which I would rate as Walter's supreme gift than the words of Plato: 'You are so far superior to Marsyas that you produce the same effect by mere words; a speech by you or even the most indifferent report of what you have said stirs us to the depths and casts a spell over us.' I miss him for that marvellous felicity, and his human warmth.

12

HOLIDAYS ON MULL

Caroline Hamilton

FATHER'S FIRST MEMORY of Scotland was that of visiting Edinburgh Castle with his parents as a four-year-old. He enjoyed a few family holidays there subsequently, but it was not until his late twenties that his passionate love of the West Highlands, which became such an integral part of his life, was aroused following a number of walking and touring holidays with James Duff.

From 1943 his visits revolved around the Shaw Stewart family at Traigh in Arisaig. He rented for some years the Gatehouse there and was treated very much as one of the mildly eccentric and haphazard family. Having been an only child, brought up with just books as companions in a fairly sheltered atmosphere in London, this association very likely contributed initially to his subsequent desire to spend as much time as possible on the West Coast. 'Only seventy-three more days,' he would utter in his lugubrious tones shortly after the beginning of a term, frequently to the surprise of whoever he was speaking to. Only then might they realise that he enjoyed ticking off the days to the next holiday quite as much as any of his children.

There is no doubt that the whole romance of the Highlands greatly appealed to Father, for he was much more of a romantic man than might have been immediately apparent. Romance for him in this sense encompassed not just the scenery, which in a way was curiously like his own nature, with its rugged simplicity and occasional volcanic outbursts. He also revelled in the company of the West Highlanders and in their particular eccentricities. How he laughed, for instance, at the recollection of Neil McGillivray, who looked after our house, claiming to have taken a shovel to clear snow off chests of drawers in the bedrooms. He never forgot the garageman coming to give his 'diag-nosis' on an ailing vehicle or the complaint one year of 'it's been terrible dry'. These were all favourite anecdotes, as indeed was the lack of a second-class mail service at Oban because there were 'no fa-ceelities for delaying the post', and the Mallaig fish-shop having to close down because customers would keep bothering its proprietors. Father's stories, however, were emphatically not borne out of any disrespect for the locals, for quite clearly he was greatly honoured to be accepted and indeed, respected by them. He was flattered that they enjoyed coming to our fireworks party each Hogmanay and that he was known by them as 'The Doctor'. It also meant a lot to him to be described as a 'stalwart man' when seen battling against a mighty wind in a boat which was leaking badly.

Above all, however, romance for Father meant adventure. He greatly resented the advent of large car-ferries to the Hebrides and improved communication to those parts in general, partly of course because they resulted in increased numbers of tourists, but chiefly because they were symbols of a steady decline in the adventure element of holidays there. It had been an adventure rushing through Rugby station carrying two golden retrievers overdosed with tranquillisers ('There's no antidote – just keep them on their feet!' the vet had said) and putting them, Mother and the young children on to the train there and driving through the night to meet them again as they drew into Oban. It had also been an adventure driving the car on two planks up to the point of balance, jamming on the brakes, and then carefully releasing them again, to roll on to the small *Lochinvar* which used to ply between Mull and the mainland, and took three cars on the deck if they weren't too large. And in later years, it could scarcely have been less exciting seeing the car swung up by winch from the pier to the ferry. It amused Father that for some years afterwards, the crew would point sadly to the dent where the car had been 'squeezed'.

That is not to say that adventures with Father on Mull ended with the dawn of the M1. In particular, the sixteen-foot clinker-built boat from which we hunted lobster and mackerel was a source of considerable excitement. I don't think that Mother ever really trusted him to behave responsibly after they, Neil McGillivray and the three small boys were forced to row back by moonlight for some hours following engine failure a few miles offshore. Whilst in the boat, Mother was always very wary of waves thereafter, particularly since Father never seemed to be wholly aware of where he was going and did seem often to steer directly towards rocks. There were moments even when the boat itself seemed to assume control. Given Mother's probably justified nervousness, Father occasionally instructed his juvenile crew that on no account were we to report back certain incidents. One such occasion was the day we decided, at his suggestion, to relive his shark-fishing days with Gavin Maxwell by running up alongside, and repeatedly prodding with the boat-hook, a basking shark at least the length of the boat. Another occasion was when he absent-mindedly knocked me fifteen feet down on to rocks where we moored the boat.

Nor was this absent-mindedness simply reserved for the family. A friend has written: 'My first recollection of Walter comes from a family holiday on Mull when we joined the Hamiltons for a picnic lunch on a sandy beach. Half the party got there by sea in their small boat. As we came in to the beach we passed a little rock, shaped like an egg, which stuck blatantly out of the sea some twenty yards offshore. Having made fast the anchor and unloaded us children, Walter, who was in charge of the motor, somehow got it jammed in gear. The boat set off full-throttle to the limit of the anchor-rope and then, following the circumference of its tether, headed for the rock. Walter was wrestling with the motor and was perhaps unaware of the danger; anyway, with an impressive crash his boat almost scaled the rock and tottered upon it. Only after another friend had waded up to her waist to his assistance, did Walter somehow manage to wobble the boat back into the sea and amazingly it was not holed.'

For as long as 'adventures' continued, Father was happy. When he was older and less able to instigate and participate in escapades I think that he probably enjoyed the Highlands, and life in general, less. Nevertheless, he never stopped loving the West Coast deeply and given this love it was not surprising that he should want to nurture the same in his family.

I don't even know whether he would have married Mother had she not taken to the Highlands. As it was, on her very first visit to Scotland, and staying with him, it rained unceasingly for three weeks. 'When Jane came to Traigh' (pronounced 'try') was a phrase which occasionally raised eyebrows but was also one which coincidentally probably conveyed the true test with which she was faced! Perhaps his having driven through a pouring wet night to Glasgow to meet her off the night train from London, after an absence from each other of some months, did something to aid her endurance.

Fortunately for me they did get married shortly after that visit and, in 1953 when the Shaw Stewarts said that they would like the Gatehouse for their own family, they bought a house of their own on Mull. Various houses were advertised in the *Oban Times* and Father and the Bursar of Westminster who happened to be staying, went over to look at one of them.

It turned out to be unsuitable and to make matters worse

they had had a puncture on the way there. However, while waiting for the puncture to be mended, they heard from the owner of the garage that there was a house in Dervaig which had been on the market for four years. Never one to hang around, Father hired a car and went straight off to see it. It proved to be the perfect family house, and after Mother had given her approval, a few weeks later on the way back to Westminster through Edinburgh, they stopped in the street outside the solicitor's office and bought Ardbeg there and then. The family moved in the following year and didn't leave until 1980.

People used to ask Father what we did on Mull. 'Oh we just exist,' he said. Certainly, in the Christmas and Easter holidays a lot of time was spent keeping warm, eating and sleeping. Ardbeg was very basic, with no central heating and the minimum of furniture. It was a large, airy house and only the kitchen and sitting-room had any potential for warmth. In one was a coal-fired Aga, upon which one could sit *in extremis*, and in the other was a large log-fire which was carefully tended by Father poking it at intervals from the comfort of his armchair. Sometimes we played Hearts or Oh Hell, using cowrie shells as counters, but mostly while indoors, we read. Winter evenings, in particular, in the Highlands are very long and those hours which we all spent deep in our books around the fire were a definite pleasure. If beds did not matter much, therefore, armchairs had to be comfortable.

Father devoured books: he seemed to enjoy reading almost anything. One moment he might have been buried in a classical text, the next in Dick Francis or Jeffrey Archer. More likely, however, he was rereading P.G. Wodehouse for the nth time, silently rocking with laughter and with tears in his eyes, as yet again he revelled in the antics of Bertie Wooster *et al*. He tried to introduce me to the joys of Wodehouse when I was about five or six by reading me

195

selected short stories. I adore the same stories now but the humour was lost on me then ('What a childish name for a book: *Eggs, Beans and Crumpets,*' I thought). Consistently therefore, as Father convulsed with giggles and was unable to continue reading, I remember staring stony-faced and, at one point, even becoming seriously concerned for his sanity.

Mull was an ideal place to spend a childhood, with our lives focused around long school holidays there. It was at Ardbeg that we were a family (boarding schools intervening during term time) and it was there – walking, fishing, bathing and generally messing about – that we enjoyed a blissful outdoor life.

For me, each holiday began in the same way: packing the car. This in itself was the product of some days' work beforehand (Mother had a list of three or four days' worth of tasks at one stage) since it was no mean feat to pack up four children, an au pair girl, two large dogs and enough equipment to aid daily life for up to six weeks. Frequently, the au pair and at least one child would travel by train to be met at Oban, but it was still a fair squash.

There was always a row packing the car. During the process, Father would be certain to accuse at least one of us of bringing unnecessary clutter and then, at the last minute, Mother would appear carrying a large box of food or a Kenwood mixer. Personally I blame Father's large briefcase which was an impossible shape, for the difficulties, but neverthless somehow everything was usually squeezed in.

The journey involved two long days' driving and a stay overnight with friends on the way. We would then catch the ferry fron Oban to Craignure and drive another hour to Dervaig. Finally, very tired, we would eat poached eggs and ham from a large joint which we had brought with us, and then be packed off to bed.

For the first week after we had arrived, Father would read for almost the whole day. He took very little notice of what was going on about him (quite an achievement with at one time three small boys milling around) until gradually he revived and began to come alive again. He would then be ready for the stimulus of visitors.

No holiday for him was complete without the company of others. All sorts came to stay, young and old – old undergraduate friends, previous and current colleagues, senior boys from Rugby and Westminster, Magdalene undergraduates and friends of us children to name but a few – and all were treated with enormous hospitality, for Father loved entertaining. In return, friends were expected to behave as one of the family and to participate in whatever was on, including wallpapering. They were also to enjoy themselves and above all to appreciate their surroundings.

As master of the anecdote, Father was of course skilled in spotting comedy. He was not a great tease as such, but he did take a certain delight in the modest discomfort of others. There was no question, for instance, but that all the oldest and least waterproof oilskins and gumboots should be reserved for visitors' use. As the steady drizzle persisted on sea-fishing trips, one could see the dampness entering the poor souls' every limb; and they were all too polite to mention it. Equally, if he did not want to see someone, Father was not averse quite simply to running away. Once at Traigh, on hearing that a bore was advancing, he and Mother and some guests who were staying fled upstairs to hide under the beds. Their game of cards was mysteriously abandoned on a table downstairs, only to be discovered by their foe on his entry into the house. Another occasion was during a trip to Coll, where, heavily disguised in a hat and large sunglasses, Father passed within inches of a public school chaplain whom he particularly disliked.

Sometimes a guest who was felt to have behaved badly was immortalised for years to come. Witness, for instance, the unfortunate young man who was discovered to have been hoarding oyster-shells under his girlfriend's plate in order to disguise the real number he had eaten; or the family upon whom lobster sandwiches were wasted; or the Rugby boy who spent a whole week curled up on the sofa with bare feet.

On other occasions, guests were able to keep Father amused for some days before they actually arrived. If he had not met them, he was liable to fantasise about what they might be like, and even if they were old friends, he might speculate about how they might react to particular situations. He once anticipated a charming and perfectly ordinarily proportioned girl to be a Ten Ton Tessie, for whom only certain pieces of furniture would be large enough but who fortunately, through the laws of physics, would require only a small amount of precious bath-water. He chuckled for years too at the thought of another girl's likely reaction when told by Charles on the way to Ardbeg, 'Don't worry about Father. He can hardly string one word after another any more!'

Another source of almost habitual speculation for us all was Mrs Browne. Mrs Browne was an ample, middle-aged woman from Wentworth who came to live in a square modern house on the edge of Dervaig. Nobody knew why she had come to Mull, and she certainly never really fitted into the local scene. Father insisted that we believe that back home she had been secretary to the ladies' golf club and, of course, a doyenne of Berkshire bring and buys. I don't think that any of us ever actually exchanged a word with her – and after a time it became important not to, otherwise we might have shattered the perfect image of her life which we had so carefully built up in endless gleeful conversations. Father's speculations reached fever-pitch one summer, following the discovery of the poor woman's clearly labelled front-door keys, not in the village street or anywhere else innocuous, but in *our* potato patch! What had she been doing? We never discovered, but the fantastical explanations which we concocted never ceased. For years, the keys were lodged in the front of the Land Rover, waiting for an appropriate moment for Father to confront her. Of course, that moment never came, and instead whenever we passed her or her house, the sound of small children's voices could be heard floating out of the open back of the car, giggling and passing judgement on the incident time and time again. Although there perhaps was one, we never wanted to believe that there was an innocent explanation – it would have ruined all our fun.

The Land Rover we had was more of a toy than a necessity. It was an eccentric machine, with rust having removed the floor on the passenger side and a horn which, after failing to work at all for many years, became liable to go off loudly at any time, even while the vehicle was parked in Tobermory High Street. As children, the discomfort of legs being perpetually soaked by wet dogs in the back was amply compensated for by the thrill of riding outside on the bars at the rear. Later also, Father taught us to drive it on the long white beach at Calgary.

He undoubtedly enjoyed these lessons, which included negotiating at speed the myriad of rabbit-holes which infested the dunes, but for Father the real joy of the Land Rover was the mud gears. He was never so happy as when grinding through some impossible terrain, three out of the four wheels spinning, mud and water spraying everywhere and a precipice looming. If she was there, Mother would usually insist that the family disembark, leaving him to battle alone while we stood and watched, waiting either for triumph or disaster. Like any small child, I was not given to criticising my parents' behaviour, but once, realising that Father was going to attempt a hopelessly boggy, near vertical slope on the edge of Loch Frisa, I remember thinking, 'This is bound to end in tears. How can he be so stupid?'

The worst of it was that I was right. Within minutes, the

Land Rover was well and truly stuck, and with the nearest farm some six miles away, many hours had passed and darkness had fallen before a tractor and a number of strong men finally arrived to help us haul it out again.

Our principal activities on Mull were walking and fishing. As far as walking was concerned, Father liked long or difficult walks best, not because he found the exercise particularly pleasurable in itself, but because they were a challenge. He also liked walks with a purpose, such as mushroom-gathering expeditions, or trips to the beach to give the dogs a swim.

Sometimes if the weather was nice we took a picnic to the beach and then all bathed as well. Father was not a natural picnicker – 'Now where is Walter going to sit?' was a well-known phrase – and he was probably not a natural swimmer either. However, he did enjoy floating on his back like a whale, with his pipe still in his mouth and the dogs swimming all around.

His enjoyment must only have been enhanced by the fact of being able to stand up to Mother and her special thermometer. This meant that he only bathed when the water was warm enough, while the rest of us by contrast, would be hurried in whatever. 'Nonsense, it's 54! Of course it's not cold!' Only after we had stripped off, would Mother reveal that she was not going in herself, at which point it was usually too late for us to turn back. Father, on the other hand, confined himself on such occasions to throwing his walking-stick endlessly for the dogs to retrieve from the sea, and then sending one of us out to get it when they failed to find it. Mother used to tease him that he loved his dogs more than his children and I sometimes wondered if that was true. Quite clearly they could do no wrong.

More than anything else, however, it was lobster and mackerel fishing, interspersed with the poaching of oysters, which were the activities Father enjoyed most. Every morning, religiously, he would set out with one or more of us to go lobster potting. Enormous time would be spent, first of all discussing where along the coastline we would be most likely to catch the lobsters, and then once some unsuspecting creatures had crawled into a pot, which would be the most delicious way of eating them. Would it be lobster patties, lobster thermidor or just plain straightforward lobster? Once, someone suggested that each member of the family should have their own lobster pot, and then whoever was lucky enough to catch one would be entitled to eat it all on their own. However, so greedy were we, that this idea was rapidly rejected, since we realised that no one would trust anybody else and that we would all have to go out potting every day in order to be sure exactly who had caught what.

On many afternoons, we would set out to sea again, this time in search of mackerel. Again we would all have strong views about where we would have the most chance of success, and when best to stop trawling the spinners in favour of the mighty 'murderer', a fearsome line with sufficient hooks to catch six fish at once. On a successful trip we might achieve a total catch of up to seventy or eighty, which was more than enough both to feed us for several days and to use as bait for the lobsters. Much the most vivid memory I have of Father, is of him there, in his large tomato-coloured jersey, scales all down the front, pipe in his mouth, and with one hand on the tiller while the other clasped a writhing mackerel to his stomach.

Father loved the boat and he loved all expeditions in it. Furthermore, whereas in general he loathed all forms of machinery, the boat meant so much to him that he was prepared to be patient with its engine as he was patient with no other. Every marine engine breaks down at least once a summer, and ours was no exception. Nevertheless, Father would tinker with it calmly at the mooring for hours on end, gradually coaxing it back into action. To his great relief in later years, Simon began to assume full responsibility for it, but for as long as he remained too young, instead Neil would often be found sitting silently and loyally by Father's side. Father never despaired of the engine, and even when parts had to be sent for from Oban or Glasgow, he remained uncharacteristically optimistic as to the likelihood of their being delivered promptly.

When it came to the end of each holiday, gloom would descend upon us and no one would want to return south, least of all Father. So important was every last day to him, that we once telegraphed my school claiming to be stormbound, and thereby excusing my planned late arrival back for term.

In everything, Father loved to be unexpected. While it must, I suppose, have shaped all of our lives to have him older than average, he was so obviously always totally young at heart that it really could not have mattered less. Once on a trek up Ben Mor, Charles as a small boy said gloomily to Father, then in his fifties, 'I expect that this will be the last time you come up here.' As it happened he was correct, but it was very surprising that he was, since Father was nothing but youthful both in mind and body. Perhaps, therefore, it was simply in order to be surprising that he deliberately declined all opportunities to make a further ascent. For in all other respects, Mull brought out a spirit of adventure in Father, a spirit which was as important as all his other qualities, and one with which undoubtedly I best remember him.

13

A RECOLLECTION

Eliza Hunt

I WAS TWELVE when I first visited Ardbeg with my parents. Walter was always very nice to me and treated me like a grown-up, which, for the youngest in a rather strong-minded, bossy family, was a great comfort. I remember on that first trip to Mull him taking us out in the boat to fish, and hold in my mind the picture of him steering the boat, pipe in mouth, gentle smile. He showed me what to do with great patience, though he was certainly not as patient with his own children. After that holiday he had the plan that I should come out on my own to Mull and help look after Caroline when she was a baby and help Jane with the cooking, and after that I spent many summers up there as cook. I'd arrive on the boat or the bus and he'd be there with his hat and pipe and two or three children to collect me and I always felt happy to see him and relaxed in his company. He never frightened me as many people did at that age; he made me laugh and gave me a feeling of enormous self-worth: such was his appreciation of me, his chief concern always being to take some of the pressure off Jane, with four young children and a large house to run.

He liked visitors and stimulus and, once stimulated, would generate enormous fun. I remember a sweepstake on how many puppies Tessa, the youngest golden retriever, was going to have and the amusement that was extracted from this for days until it turned out to be a phantom pregnancy.

He always called Tessa 'a dumb blonde'; he spoiled the dogs outrageously, often taking these great soft creatures on to his lap.

My job was formally arranged with a day off a week, I think, and one of the greatest pleasures was to spend the morning with Walter sitting in the big armchairs in the sitting-room and reading. It would always surprise and comfort me that such a highly intelligent man would enjoy Mary Stewart and Georgette Heyer as I did, so I could read them without guilt. 'Nothing gives me a greater sense of sin than reading a thriller in the mornings,' he would say with glee.

As I got older and was studying for A levels and was reading Dostoevsky or *The Faerie Queene*, he would always tell me that I mustn't take life too seriously at the most fearfully serious-minded time of my life. He never made me think of him as the highly intellectual academic that he was. I often think now I could have picked his brains more – he was much cleverer than any of my teachers – but it would never have occurred to me or him. I was in Mull when my A level results arrived with three dismal grades and he said, as he handed me a strong drink, 'Why should anybody cry because they have succeeded in passing the wretched exams?'

We had lovely days, walking, fishing, swimming. Walter always had to have a chair on the beach and he didn't really like picnics. We usually had lunch and high tea at home and all my cooking was warmly appreciated. I'll never serve a steak-and-kidney pie without thinking of Walter saying how nice it would be with a few oysters in it, or the pleasure we all got when we ate the lobster or mackerel we caught. He'd come into the kitchen just before lunch, at the point when cooks are always hot and frazzled, with a sherry or even a gin for me, and I remember latterly several conversations over elevenses as to what he planned for my father's retirement. He was a great planner for the benefit of others. He started to plan what my father should do when he retired several years before the event.

He was never averse to rolling up his sleeves and washing up, and I still have a fine picture in my mind of him and my father side by side in the pantry peeling the potatoes. Sometimes he would get passionately annoyed over the pettiest thing: once because we had to stand in a queue for breakfast on a ferry trip. He didn't participate well in the hurly-burly of ordinary tourists. I remember he always called the large ferry that carried people between the Islands – the *George V* I think it was – 'that floating hell' – I can still hear him saying it with ferocious relish. I remember him getting in a fury once because one of his children did something incompetently in the boat but he never reproached me for anything. I once swore Charles and Simon to secrecy when I drove the Land Rover into a ditch (I got it out, luckily), but I think he did know about it but continued to trust me to drive his children in it and never said a word till years later. Equally, when I might have killed Caroline by tipping her out of her pram, no fuss was made. In all of this, of course, the credit goes to Jane as well; like all the happiest married couples they were a team.

Those holidays in Mull were a very happy time for me and Walter's totally unpretentious simplicity had a great in-fluence on me, I realise as I look back. I see him now on one of the rare sunny summer mornings tenderly picking the sweet peas that he grew outside the front door and bringing them in to put in a vase and I am sure that is how he would most like to be remembered.

Appendix

THREE SERMONS

W. H.

Happiness[1]

I DO NOT propose today to preach what might be called a full-blown sermon. That will perhaps be some compensation to you for having received something like a treble ration last Sunday.

There is, however, one thing that I want to say, and it arises out of a remark made to me by one of you, speaking to me about one of the boys who left Rugby a week ago. He said that he thought that his father was quite right to take him away because he was not happy here. Now that, on the face of it, is a perfectly sensible and reasonable thing to say, and in the particular circumstances to which it referred it was very likely justified. Nevertheless, it could have deeper implications, and it is about them that I want to speak very briefly.

That remark, you see, might be taken to imply that wherever one finds oneself in circumstances in which one isn't happy the only thing to do is to change the circumstances. One could not, it seems to me, follow a more mistaken principle. For one thing it may be oneself, not the circumstances, that needs changing. My own pride or egotism or jealousy or self-pity is quite as likely to be the source of my unhappiness as anything in the world outside myself, and if I am unlucky enough to have a temperament which exposes me to the domination of these emotions, I shall

---

[1]Delivered at the end of term, Rugby, 9 July 1965.

206

be unhappy wherever I am until I have by one means or another won the victory over them. So before I run away from my existing circumstances because I am unhappy, and I can assure you that a headmaster sometimes has an impulse to do so quite as strongly as any of you, I had better at least try to discover whether it is my circumstances or my own nature which is the cause of my unhappiness. 'The world is so full of a number of things, I'm sure we should all be as happy as kings,' wrote R. L. Stevenson. Perhaps we should be, but we often aren't; we can all of us think of people who are in a position to gratify their every whim, and who yet are desperately unhappy.

Of course, I am not denying for a moment that unhappiness may be the result of external circumstances. It is difficult to be happy with toothache, even though the Stoics thought that their ideal man would be; it is difficult to be happy if one is perpetually surrounded by disagreeable people; and some of you, I don't doubt, are apt to think that it is impossible to be happy if one has to live a life in which one's freedom of action is to any extent restricted. Yet even if I am convinced that my unhappiness springs from my circumstances rather than myself, there are almost certainly good reasons for making the best of things. Not to do so is likely to be totally inconsistent with the pursuit of any long-term objective whatsoever. If I am always asking myself the question 'Am I happy?', and deciding to change my circumstances whenever the answer is No, the course of my life will proceed in such violent zig-zags that it becomes quite impossible for me to reach any destination that I propose for myself. And I don't mean any necessarily very idealistic destination. My objective may be nothing more lofty than a comfortable and well-paid job, or a decent reputation, but I shall not have much chance of obtaining it if I change direction whenever I am irked by anything in the course which leads to it. And if I set before myself any higher goal such as a service to humanity or the advancement of knowledge or the cultivation of an art, the question whether what happens to me in the pursuit of that goal makes me happy or unhappy becomes simply irrelevant.

The plain fact is then that present happiness or unhappiness is not a satisfactory criterion of the value of any course we are pursuing, if only because its application is incompatible with the pursuit of any consistent course at all. The American Declaration of Independence says that all men are endowed with certain inalienable rights, and that among these are life, liberty and the pursuit of happiness. That sounds very fine, but as far as the pursuit of happiness is concerned it really will not hold water. Happiness is not something that one can pursue for itself; the more one consciously pursues it the more it eludes one's grasp. Happiness in any true sense is something that comes unsought when one is pursuing something else, and the more one is convinced of the value of that other object the greater the happiness that attends the pursuit of it. And that sort of happiness is largely unaffected by the frustrations and irritations and even the sufferings and sorrows from which no human being, whatever his circumstances, can hope to be permanently exempt; for that reason it is the only happiness really worth having, and another name for it is serenity. We all recognise it when we see it; we all know people whose serenity is not impaired in circumstances which would make most of us thoroughly miserable. All these people have one common characteristic: they are devoted to some goal or cause outside themselves, which gives them no time to take themselves too seriously and to ask themselves the fatal question 'Am I happy?'

Well, that is what I wanted to say. You may think that it is not particularly religious, but you would be wrong. This is one of the great fundamental truths about human nature verified by the universal experience of humanity and it is with truths of this kind that religion is concerned. It is in fact simply a particular application of the most important discovery that man has ever made about himself. That discovery is that 'Whosoever will save his life shall lose it, and whosoever will lose his life shall find it', which is in fact to be found in all four gospels and in some of them repeated more than once.

'As we have many members in one body and all members have not the same office; so, we, being many, are one body in Christ, and every one members one of another.' (Rom. 12:4 and 5).[2]

One of the most obvious things about human life is that it is hopelessly unfair. I say hopelessly because, although there are some spheres in which human effort can do something to correct this state of affairs, nobody can ever abolish the fundamental inequalities which exist between one human being and another in such matters as health and strength and brains and temperament and environment. And in a small way this unfairness cannot perhaps be better exemplified than in the distribution of prizes, which formed part of our proceedings in the Temple Speech Room yesterday. Take two extreme examples. X, though essentially an idle dog, is so well endowed by nature that he can hardly avoid achieving a certain amount of academic success and winning at any rate a few prizes; Y, a boy who is a shining example of every virtue, honest, willing, industrious, persevering, is so thick in the head that the highest praise he will ever win is something like this: 'Nobody can say that he doesn't try.' Now there are a good many Ys in the world and even, I am thankful to say at Rugby (in fact they considerably outnumber the Xs) and it would be no wonder if they asked themselves, as they sat in the Speech Room yesterday, what all this business of prizes and talk of scholarships had to do with *them*. It is to that question that I want in the first place today to suggest an answer.

---

[2]Delivered on Speech Day, Rugby, 26 June 1959

May I begin by drawing an illustration from an event which occurred six years ago and which thrilled even the most cynical, the climbing of Mt Everest by Sir Edmund Hillary and the Sherpa Tenzing on 19 May 1953? This great achievement of the human spirit, an achievement perhaps all the more sublime because it had, as far as one can see, very little practical significance, provides the clearest possible example, not only of men's doggedness and determination over a period of some thirty years, but of the value and indeed the absolute necessity of corporate effort. It is completely obvious that Hillary and Tenzing would never have stood on the summit of Everest but for the devoted service of a much larger number of men belonging both to their own and to previous expeditions, most of whom – and this is the point that I want particularly to emphasise – most of whom, I say, knew for certain right from the start that whoever might ultimately get to the top it would not be themselves. These men, the Ys of the party, so to speak, were content all the same to encounter extreme danger and hardship, reconnoitring, marking routes and carrying heavy loads, in order that others might have the glorious experience of reaching the top by standing, as it were, on their shoulders.

Now let us go back for a moment to our prizes and scholarships. Just as the final climb of Hillary and Tenzing was not an isolated individual feat but depended upon the united efforts of many others, so, just as truly though perhaps less obviously, the intellectual achievements which won recognition yesterday are not isolated individual feats either. What makes it possible for a few people to distinguish themselves in this particular way is the existence of the whole complex organisation of the school and its maintenance of a decent average level of attainment. To that everybody contributes who does an honest piece of work here to the best of his ability, however humble and unrewarded. It is only by the accumulation of such honest pieces of work that a soil, so to speak, is created in which the intelligence of particular individuals can take root and flourish, and the achievements which were recognised and rewarded yesterday are in a sense the achievements of all those who have contributed, very likely without any idea that they were doing so, to the creation of such a soil at Rugby.

And, of course, it is not only in intellectual matters that it is true, as my text says, that 'we are members one of another'. A school like this comprises and enfolds any number of sectional interests and loyalties, houses, societies, teams and so on. We can with some justice be proud of the breadth of our activities, of the fact that there is something for almost everybody, of the number of different things we do. But underlying all these there is the larger unity of the school itself, and that school will be in a healthy condition only if we regard the successes and failures both of individuals and of particular sections of our community, in whatever field they may lie, intellectual, artistic, athletic, or even more, as being, quite literally, and not in any metaphorical sense, the successes and failures of us all.

Still, when all is said and done, the world of school, though extremely important because what sort of people we are going to be depends to a large extent on what sort of people we have made ourselves here, the life of school is after all only a mimic world, and I want to turn finally to something of much wider and more abiding significance. My text says not only that 'we are members one of another' but also that 'we being many are one body in Christ'. All our life, whether at Rugby or afterwards, our service and our loyalty will be claimed by corporate bodies to which we shall belong, clubs and colleges, business concerns and institutions in which we work, and embracing and including all these, just as Rugby embraces and includes all the various activities which make up its life, the State of which we are citizens. All these will be affected for better or worse by the quality of the contribution which we make to them, in however humble or however distinguished a capacity. But even that is not the end of the story. As well as being citizens of an earthly kingdom we are citizens of the kingdom of God, bound to contribute whatever we may have in us to its building, and to fight as Christ's faithful soldiers and servants against the forces of evil. The contribution of most of us may probably not be very spectacular – it will not be given to most of us to stand upon the summit of Everest, and we should count ourselves lucky if we can even do anything which directly enables others to do so. Often we shall be oppressed by a feeling that the utmost our effort can achieve is so utterly insignificant as hardly to be worth while; sometimes we may even be unable to see that in doing faithfully whatever job may fall to our lot we are making any contribution to the sum of things at all. In those circumstances I should like to think that you might remember a story which I once heard treated by a famous preacher, much better than I can treat it, the story of a donkey.

You all know the story, for it is the story of Christ's entry into Jerusalem on Palm Sunday, a tumultuous procession with crowds of people cheering and crying 'Hosanna in the highest', throwing their clothes and branches of trees in the road, an ironical contrast to the procession to Calvary five days later. In all that throng there was one living creature noticed by nobody, just doing what he had been trained to do without the slightest idea what the excitement was all about, who was probably frightened by the noise and very likely couldn't see more than the ground just before his feet, and yet whose presence was absolutely indispensable, the donkey on which Jesus was riding. He had sent two of his disciples to fetch him, you will remember, as he was approaching Jerusalem, and told them to say if any one interfered with them 'The Lord hath need of him'. He was just an ordinary ass, not an ass endowed with any miraculous or extraordinary capacities like Balaam's ass in the Old Testament, who saw the angel of the Lord standing in the way and reproached his master for beating him. Just an ordinary ass, and yet to him, quite unconscious of what was happening and simply doing his accustomed job, fell the task and the honour of carrying Christ forward on his journey.

I am sure that I need not labour the application of this story. We are most of us just ordinary asses and yet 'the Lord hath need of us', and at any moment, probably without our knowing it, simply by faithfully discharging our ordinary duties and not shirking them, we too may be carrying Christ forward, we too may be contributing something indispensable, something that nobody but we can contribute, to the building of that unity in Christ of which we are members, in fact to the building of the kingdom of God.

'I found an altar with this inscription, To the unknown God. Whom therefore ye ignorantly worship, him declare I unto you.' (Acts 17:23)[3]

A preacher charged with the task of addressing you on the relevance of classical studies to Christianity may perhaps be pardoned for boggling at the enormous field before him. At every stage of development, at least down to the Middle Ages, Greek thought exercised a profound influence on Christianity, to say nothing of the influence of Christianity upon the fate of the ancient world, and it is no exaggeration to say that the Christian theology of our own times, owes at least as much to classical culture as to Judaism. To begin with, there is the obvious fact that, whatever the native tongues of its various writers, Greek is the language of the New Testament, and to this day Latin is the language employed in worship in a by no means inconsiderable part of the universal church. Or consider for a moment the contrast presented by any of the synoptic gospels and the Nicene Creed, the one a sublime yet simple narrative of Christ's life and report of his teaching, in which the underlying beliefs are assumed rather than formulated, the other a statement of a series of dogmatic and largely abstract propositions, wholly unethical, on the relations subsisting between the persons of the Trinity. That contrast is a measure of the influence exerted upon Christianity by Greek philosophy in the first three centuries, for this shift of emphasis from the facts of Christ's earthly life and teaching to the philosophical and theological implications of those facts was the result of the transplantation of Christianity from Semitic to Greek soil,

---

[3]Delivered at Magdalene, Cambridge, 15 May 1949.

and of the exposure to the speculative and systematising intellect of the Greeks of beliefs which for the first apostles were matters either of simple intuition or of revelation. Again, a thousand years later, when the medieval schoolmen set out to construct a philosophical system which should integrate Christian doctrine into the sum of human knowledge, it was to the metaphysics of Aristotle that they turned for their framework, and in the last resort it is Aristotle who is chiefly responsible for the form taken of what is still the official philosophy of the Roman Catholic Church. In fact, if Jewry is the cradle of Christianity, Greece is its foster-mother.

But such themes as these are as far beyond my competence as they are beyond the limits of my time, and I will ask your attention merely for a single point, suggested by the lesson which has just been read and from which I have taken my text. When Paul was at Athens 'certain philosophers of the Epicureans and of the Stoics encountered him'. What religious beliefs did they bring to the encounter? Some sort of answer to this question is accessible to a student of the Classics, and will serve to illustrate the essential nature of Christianity, and to show both by likeness and by contrast what precisely was the new thing which it brought into the world.

In a broad sense Epicureanism and Stoicism may be said to have divided between them the allegiance of such educated and thinking men in the time of Christ as were not pure sceptics. Both had arisen in the fourth century BC as philosophies of resignation, designed to alleviate the spiritual discomfort of the individual soul, torn loose by the political upheavals begun by Alexander from the intimate solidarity of the city-state. There the good life had been the life of the good citizen, an ideal easy to grasp and not too difficult to attain; now the individual, 'a stranger and afraid, in a world he never made', was left to fend for himself in a universe immensely enlarged by the removal of the old cosy barriers, and the disappearance of the familiar and comfortable, even if only half-believed, pieties of city-state religion.

At first sight the comfort provided by Epicurus and Zeno, the Stoic, seems cold enough. With Epicurus we need hardly concern ourselves; he had nothing to recommend but the pursuit of pleasure, albeit a refined and cultivated pleasure, a conclusion based upon a simple and dogmatic materialism; his system remained fixed and unchanging from the time of its founder, and its adherents, comparatively few in number, can only have greeted the preaching of the gospel with a stare of blank incomprehension. Not theirs the ignorant worship of the unknown God, for the simple reason that they worshipped no god at all.

With the Stoic Zeno it is very different. He too is a materialist, but for him the individual soul is akin to what he calls God, because it is a detached portion of the fiery essence which interpenetrates and controls the whole universe. But none the less his is a cheerless creed. The whole duty of a man is 'to live according to nature', that is, to accommodate his will and desires to the impersonal force at work in the universe, whose decrees know no shadow of turning. It is in fact pure fatalism, and its professors, who strive by subduing the desires of the world and the flesh to bring themselves into conformity with the course of nature, which they must in any case follow, are inspired by no hope and no reward. The situation of the Stoic believer is summed up in the words of the famous prayer of Cleanthes, Zeno's pupil.

> Lead me, O Zeus and thou, Necessity,
> To whatsoever destiny you will.
> I follow fearless, or, if I rebel
> And will not follow, I must follow still.

Renunciation for renunciation's sake seems an even less inspiring ideal than the refined pleasure of Epicurus, but it found a congenial soil in the austere and strenuous Roman

217

character of the Republic and attracted far more adherents. Nevertheless, in the three centuries which separated Zeno from Christ, Stoicism underwent a significant change of tone. The god, who for Zeno is nothing but eternal law, tends in some later Stoics to be represented as a watchful providence, a moral and spiritual being, even a loving father, in spite of the fact that such a development is quite inconsistent with the fundamental principles of Stoic physical philosophy.

The change which I speak of may be abundantly illustrated from the writings of Seneca. Forget for a moment that Seneca was the tutor and minister of Nero, and an accessory, even if an unwilling accessory, in his crimes, but bear in mind that he was an almost exact contemporary of Paul; his pupil became emperor in the year 54, the very year in which Paul spoke on Mars Hill. What has Seneca to say of his god? Something like this, if I may be allowed to paraphrase and condense him. 'God guides us by his providence, embraces all by his love, his goodness is as boundless as his power, and we can best worship him by imitating his goodness. We are all, both slave and free, children of one father, and our duty is to live for others.' 'We are all more or less bad, and we should be gentle to one another.' Or take the much nobler Phrygian ex-slave Epictetus, with his doctrine that human life begins and ends in God, and his interpretation of Cleanthes' prayer:

> Dare to lift up your eyes to God and to say:
> 'Do with me henceforth as thou wilt; I am of one mind with thee, I am thine; I ask not to escape any of the things that thou hast appointed for me.'

Do we not catch here the echo of another prayer 'Nevertheless not what I will but what thou wilt?' If this is the unknown god whose altar Paul saw on the Areopagus, he is a god some of whose features at least we recognise. In what sense then does Paul speak of him as still unknown?

I believe that it is true that from a time at least as far back as Socrates and Plato, with their conviction that it is better to suffer wrong than to do wrong, a few of the best minds of Greece and Rome had reached for themselves an ideal in ethics, and even a conception of the nature of God, not impossibly distant, indeed quite recognisably akin, to the ideals of Christianity. In what then, you may ask, does the originality and inspiration of Christianity consist? Surely in this. The almost Christian piety of Seneca or Epictetus or Marcus Aurelius has really no solid basis or justification; it is, as I have said, the product of a revolution inconsistent with the basic principles of Stoicism; in fact it is no more than the expression of a natural craving in the human heart to worship something other than a cold abstraction. We may see in it an indication that a process was at work in the pagan world parallel to that process of gradual enlightenment and preparation among the Jews which it is commonplace to find in the Old Testament. But the love and providence of God could not be demonstrated and made palpable. They remained no more than hypothetical and in consequence powerless to inspire more than a handful of philosophical souls, till God revealed himself in Christ, and gave form and substance, or, if one may say so flesh and blood, to what had hitherto been no more than wishful thinking. The more clearly we recognise an affinity between the ethics of the later Stoics and the ethics of Christianity, or even between their two conceptions of the nature of God, the more clearly we shall see also in what the essence of Christianity consists. It lies not in the acceptance of a new moral code, even that of the Sermon on the Mount, or in the completion of a fresh stage in man's search into the nature of divinity, but in the crucifixion and resurrection of the Son of God. It is what Christ was and did and suffered, not what he said, that make Christianity a new thing, by revealing in his mighty acts God

219

coming down to save man, instead of man striving by searching to find out God.

That is why all through the apostles' preaching the emphasis is almost entirely on the death and resurrection of Christ. Consider once more Paul's speech at Athens; in all that he says, not least in his insistence on the brotherhood of man, in support of which he quotes a Stoic poet, Aratus, 'for we are also his offspring', he is in full accord with Stoic teaching, until he comes to his closing words: 'He will judge the world in righteousness by that man whom he hath ordained; whereof he hath given assurance unto all men, *in that he hath raised him from the dead.*' The words at once destroy any comfortable illusion that Christianity is even the same in kind as the religion of Paul's audience. 'When they heard of the resurrection of the dead, some mocked.' We are not told that the mockers were exclusively Epicurean. Some no doubt were Stoics, to whom for all their talk about the love of God, a God who shows that love in action by coming down from heaven and being made man is inconceivable. 'We preach Christ crucified,' Paul wrote to the Corinthians, 'unto the Jews a stumbling-block and unto the Greeks foolishness; but unto them that are called, both Jews and Greeks, Christ the power of God and the wisdom of God. Because the foolishness of God is wiser than men, and the weakness of God is stronger than men.' That is the point about which it is no good deceiving ourselves.

If we learn nothing else from a study of classical thought in the first century, we can at least carry away a conviction of a truth which is often much obscured in our own day by a timid and ineffectual humanism, which attempts to reduce Christianity to a code of moral precepts with no miraculous implications. Had it been only that it would have had no more vitality than the Stoicism from which it would have hardly been distinguishable; it is because it is the gospel of Christ crucified and risen and fundamentally nothing else at all that it is not a theoretical philosophy for a few chosen intellects but a universal religion or way of life for mankind.

I have attempted very imperfectly and summarily to show one way in which some knowledge of the thought of Greece and Rome sheds light on the essential nature of the gospel. To declare that gospel is the main business of a preacher, perhaps a layman and a classic, but in such an address as this I may also ask you to do honour to those *animae naturaliter Christianae* in the pagan world who without the light of revelation came so near to the spirit of Christ. To them also may be applied what is said in the Epistle to the Hebrews of the worthies of the Old Testament: 'They that say such things declare plainly that they seek a country. And truly, if they had been mindful of that country from whence they came out they might have had opportunity to have returned. But now they desire a better country, that is, an heavenly; wherefore God is not ashamed to be called their God; for he hath prepared for them a city.'

Those who assisted were:

Eric Anderson	Peter Lawrence
Robert Armstrong	Donald Lindsay
Dennis Babbage	Stephen Lushington
Simon Barrington-Ward	Henry Maas
Robert Bourne	John Mackay
Wilfred Bourne	Robin Macnaghten
Pauline Burnet	Stephen and Mary McWatters
Simon Burrows	Nicholas Montagu
Janet Carleton	John Morrison
James Cobban	Denis Moylan
Brian Dance	Denis Murphy
Brian Deakin	Angus Nicholson
Michael Dias	Richard Ollard
Patrick Duff	William Ollard
John Evans	Raef Payne
Tom Faber	Thomas Pearce
Charles Fletcher	Peter Petrie
Geoffrey Foxcroft	Hubert Picarda
Stephen Freer	Jim Pitts-Tucker
Janet Friedlander	Adrian Poole
Guy Furnivall	Enoch Powell
Michael Goulder	Adolf Prag
Edna Graham	James Ramsden
John Graham	George Ramsden
David Graham-Campbell	Francis and Joyce Rawes
Christopher Greenwood	Theo Redpath
Archie and Sheelagh Hardie	Harry Sandbach
Peter Hare	Rivers Scott
Ronald Harrison	Jackie Shaw Stewart
Geoffrey Helliwell	David Simpson
David Hirst	Philip Snow
Ronald Hope-Jones	John Sweet
Ronald Hyam	Timothy Tosswill
Eliza Hunt	John Tyson
James Hunt	Oliver Van Oss
Douglas Hurd	Peter Walker
Charles Impey	Andrew Wallace-Hadrill
Ted Kenney	Lewis Webster
Richard Kindersley	John Wilson
Tim Kirkup	Brian Young
Robert Latham	Theo Zinn